3rd Edition

Advanced

MARKET LEADER

Business English Practice File

John Rogers

Unit 2

Unit 5

unit 9

unit 7

unit 8

First impressions

A Complete the second sentence in each pair so that it has approximately the same meaning as the first sentence. Use between *two* and *five* words, including the word given, and a word related to one of the words in the first sentence.

1 Sue is very experienced in giving PowerPoint presentations. (**considerable**)

Sue *has considerable experience of* giving PowerPoint presentations.

2 The presenter failed to emphasise the benefits of the reforms. (**place**)

The presenter failed to .... the benefits of the reforms.

3 I have arranged for our guests to be met at the airport. (**made**)

I have .... our guests to be met at the airport.

4 As far as I know, the seminar has been postponed. (**best**)

To ...., the seminar has been postponed.

5 Could you briefly summarise the main points of the meeting for us? (**brief**)

Could you give .... of the main points of the meeting?

6 They plan to publish the report next month. (**scheduled**)

The report .... next month.

7 The debate was hastily concluded. (**hasty**)

The debate was brought to ....

8 Do you think you could guide me a bit on how to structure my speech? (**some**)

Do you think you could .... on how to structure my speech?

9 These reforms will significantly reduce government spending. (**significant**)

These reforms will make .... government spending.

10 We bought these laser jet printers to replace our old dot matrix ones. (**as**)

We bought these laser jet printers .... our old ones.

11 Ms Wilkinson heads the Human Resources department. (**of**)

Ms Wilkinson is .... the Human Resources department.

B Cross out the word which does not normally go with the keyword in the bubble.

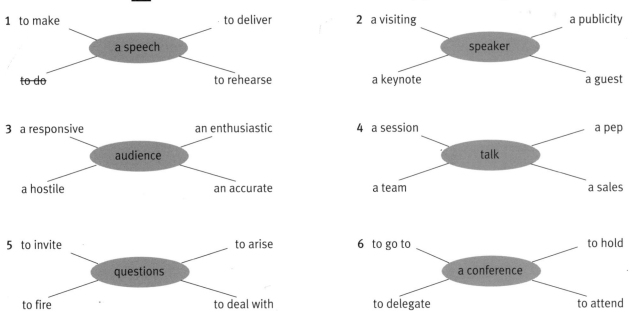

1 to make / to deliver / **a speech** / ~~to do~~ / to rehearse

2 a visiting / a publicity / **speaker** / a keynote / a guest

3 a responsive / an enthusiastic / **audience** / a hostile / an accurate

4 a session / a pep / **talk** / a team / a sales

5 to invite / to arise / **questions** / to fire / to deal with

6 to go to / to hold / **a conference** / to delegate / to attend

WORD POWER

C Complete the sentences with the correct form of a collocation from Exercise B.

1 ....Rehearsing........ his ..speech........ for three days before the conference had greatly boosted his self-confidence.

2 The task of .... is often to introduce the theme of a conference and give the main talk.

3 Just because people did not clap frantically does not mean that you had ....

4 The aim of .... is to encourage and energise the audience.

5 The audience had been rather quiet so I did not expect them .... at me at the end of my talk.

6 We are pleased to announce that our next .... will be .... in May.

D Complete each sentence with the best word.

1 It is a good idea to make eye contact with your audience but you should avoid ....b........ .

   a) watching   b) staring   c) peeping

2 In some cultures, when people seem to .... their heads in agreement, it does not necessarily mean that they agree with you.

   a) nod   b) lean   c) fold

3 I felt rather tired during the talk and my mind soon began to ....

   a) slouch   b) wander   c) distract

4 I .... into an old friend at the conference. I hadn't seen him for ages.

   a) crashed   b) flowed   c) bumped

5 The manager had allegedly been involved in .... dealings with cash payments in brown envelopes.

   a) sleazy   b) referral   c) selfless

6 A presenter needs to think about .... : for example, the way they stand, the way in which they can be upright but not rigid, the way they take charge of the space.

   a) gesture   b) posture   c) figure

A **Complete the article below with some of the sentences a–h. You will only need six of the eight sentences.**

a) A presentation cannot be successful unless it takes the needs and interests of the audience into account.

b) Having a clear objective in view enables you to map out the most convenient route to get to your destination.

c) Once you have established that, you can prioritise your material.

d) In addition, make sure you plan carefully how you are going to introduce yourself.

e) It will also affect the manner in which we choose to deliver our talk.

f) Most presenters feel more relaxed if they have had the opportunity to go to the conference venue beforehand.

g) Of course, it is better to plan in advance when you want to deal with questions.

h) With such information, you can tailor both the style and the content of your talk to your audience's expectations.

PREPARING FOR YOUR PRESENTATION

What you really need to think about before you face your audience

Before you actually get down to the nitty-gritty of planning the presentation itself, you need to reflect on a number of crucial questions. First of all, ask yourself what exactly your aim is. ......b......[1] You can then decide how many stages are necessary to get there, what the aim of each individual stage is and how each one contributes to your overall aim. ....[2] In other words, you can sift the essential data from the rest and get rid of any irrelevant or unnecessary detail.

However, content and structure are not everything. The talks we give are not just about a certain topic, they also have a specific purpose. Talks may be delivered in order to convey information, to persuade, to spur people into action or for countless other reasons. Obviously, the purpose of our talk will have a significant effect on the language we use. ....[3] Although the importance of clear aims cannot be overstated, most experienced presenters seem to agree that it is only secondary to the human factor.

Which brings us to the second question we should all be asking ourselves at the planning stage: Who are the audience? ....[4] What you say has to be appropriate not only to your aim but also to your audience.

Therefore, it is always a good idea to find out as much as you can about the audience well before you face them. ....[5] You can also anticipate how much they already know about your topic and so pitch your talk at the right level.

Finally, never underestimate the importance of the physical environment in which you will deliver your talk. ....[6] Walking around the room where your talk is going to be will help you focus on your audience rather than on your surroundings. This also gives you the chance to check that all the equipment you need is there and is in working order.

B Insert (^) each of the adverbs 1–8 in the corresponding underlined text in the article below.

1 absolutely

2 actively

3 actually

4 afterwards

5 badly

6 barely

7 forever

8 physically

The careerist: First impressions

Why are first impressions so important?

Corinne Mills, Managing Director of Personal Career Management, explains that people do not just hold on to first impressions, they also seek to reinforce them[1]. 'If you make a good first impression, people will look for the best in you. If you make a bad or indifferent first impression, you have to work so much harder[2].'

How should I prepare?

'It's all visual to start off with,' says Ms Mills. 'You need a look that is contemporary and appropriate – if you're starting a new job, then this is the time to get a new suit and a new haircut. If you look up-to-date, others will believe that your ideas and thinking are up-to-date; people do make these assumptions.'

Louise Mowbray, a personal branding consultant, says you need to ensure you are relaxed[3]. 'Body language doesn't lie: ensure you're relaxed when you meet someone – and make sure you don't have to run to meetings.'

How should I behave?

'Treat people as though they are your peers,' advises Ms Mills. 'Don't be too deferential or cocky. Have a sense of self.'

What are the main pitfalls?

You need to be authentic. Unrealistic embellishments will not help your confidence and can create future problems. 'Don't put yourself in a position where you're having to cover up[4],' says Ms Mowbray.

Finally, remember that good manners go a long way – so do not take mobile phone calls unless you have to[5].

What if things are going[6]?

'It's worth asking the other person,' says Ms Mills. 'Say something like, "Am I missing something?"' This, she explains, shows both confidence and sensitivity. 'I had a client who had a job interview with a chief executive who looked at him[7]. After a while, he asked, "Is something wrong?" and the guy said, "Didn't anyone tell you before you came in? My father just died." After that, the interview went okay and he got the job[8].'

A **Match the informal phrases 1–6 with the formal phrases a–f.**

1 Because of ...

2 Can you tell us more about ... ?

3 Here are ...

4 I've got some bad news.

5 What exactly do you need?

6 I've got some good news.

a) Please find enclosed ...

b) Please let us know your exact requirements.

c) We regret to inform you that ...

d) Owing to ...

e) We are pleased to inform you that ...

f) We would be grateful if you could send us further information about ...

B **The e-mail below is inappropriate because it uses an informal writing style. Rewrite it completely using the formal phrases in the box to replace the underlined items.**

> attend the event
>
> if you could confirm your talk at your earliest convenience
>
> We are writing to inform you
>
> With best wishes
>
> We would be honoured
>
> Please do not hesitate to contact me
>
> We realise this is a topic close to your own heart
>
> should you require further details
>
> We would be extremely grateful

From:	Frances Reynolds
To:	Dieter Fuchs
Date:	18th September
Subject:	Conference: Beyond Culture Shock

Dear Mr Fuchs,

This is just to let you know[1] that the Chamber of Commerce in Birmingham is hosting a one-day event early next month on the subject of 'Beyond Culture Shock'.

We know this is the kind of stuff you are interested in[2] following the recent merger of the Savings Bank of Salzburg with the Midlands Savings Bank and the intercultural issues that subsequently arose. It would be great[3] if you could come[4] and give a plenary talk to the business community at large.

Thanks in advance[5] for letting us know as soon as possible if you can make it[6]. Please find attached a speaker's proposal form. Just get in touch with me[7] if you need more information[8].

All the best[9],

Frances Reynolds
Events Manager
Birmingham Chamber of Commerce
franreynolds@msb.co.uk

C **Work out the difference between the sentences in each pair.**

1 We need a radical management shake-up.
What we need is a radical management shake-up.

2 I really liked the way she kept in touch with her audience.
It was the way she kept in touch with her audience **that I really liked**.

D **Rewrite the sentences in the same way as in Exercise C.**

1 I'm looking forward to a good networking function.

2 They don't like slang or colloquialisms.

3 Your rapport with the audience matters most.

4 I didn't like the sort of questions they asked me.

5 They expect a high-tech presentation.

E ◀)) 1 **Listen to the different presenters and decide what each one is doing.**

• Write one letter (**a–f**) next to the number of the speaker.

• You will have to use some letters twice.

Speaker 1 ....   a) introducing the main topic

Speaker 2 ....   b) turning to a new topic

Speaker 3 ....   c) going back to a previous point

Speaker 4 ....   d) referring to visuals

Speaker 5 ....   e) dealing with questions

Speaker 6 ....   f) concluding the presentation

Speaker 7 ....

Speaker 8 ....

F ◀)) 2 **Listen to the examples. Notice where / t / and / d / tend to disappear.**

1 Pleased to meet you.

2 Our website's just been updated.

3 Sorry, I didn't quite catch your last point.

Explanation

In rapid speech, / t / and / d / often disappear when they are between two other consonants. This is called *elision*. An awareness of elision can help you understand rapid speech better.

G **Cross out the letters in these sentences that may disappear during rapid speech.**

1 It's hard to say which aspects are the most positive.

2 The second talk focused particularly on deregulation.

3 Last summer we worked together on a research project.

4 The first presentation wasn't very difficult to understand.

5 I wouldn't say it was the greatest networking event I've ever attended.

◀)) 3 **Listen and check your answers. Then listen again and practise the sentences.**

Training

A Match the nouns 1–6 with the nouns a–f to make common compounds.

1 professional   a) building
2 work   b) development
3 vocational   c) training
4 team   d) placement
5 performance   e) resources
6 human   f) appraisal

B Complete the clues with a compound from Exercise A.

1 It is about your growth as an employee. = *professional development*
2 It teaches you the skills you need to do a particular job. = ...
3 It is an opportunity to evaluate your work and to get feedback. = ...
4 It is similar to an internship. = ...
5 It means the same as 'personnel'. = ...
6 It helps people work more efficiently together. = ...

C Cross out the word which does not normally go with the keyword in the bubble.

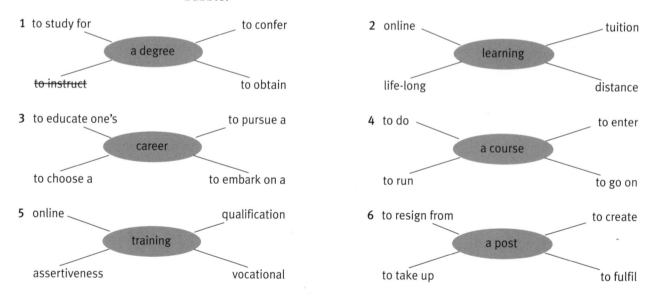

1 to study for   to confer — *a degree* — ~~to instruct~~   to obtain

2 online   tuition — *learning* — life-long   distance

3 to educate one's   to pursue a — *career* — to choose a   to embark on a

4 to do   to enter — *a course* — to run   to go on

5 online   qualification — *training* — assertiveness   vocational

6 to resign from   to create — *a post* — to take up   to fulfil

D Complete the sentences with the correct form of a collocation from Exercise C.

1 An honorary *degree was conferred* on her by Harvard in 2003.
2 .... is the activity of seeking out new knowledge or developing a skill and participating in educational activities until retirement and beyond.
3 What advice would you give to a person .... in your field of work or study?
4 The Business Institute .... a part-time MBA .... since 1999.
5 .... helps you behave and express your opinions more confidently.
6 Owing to an unexpected surge in demand, we have had to .... ten new ....

E Complete this crossword puzzle.

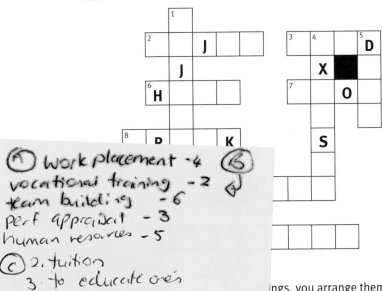

Handwritten note:
Ⓐ Work placement - 4   Ⓑ
vocational training - 2
team building - 6
perf appraisal - 3
human resources - 5
Ⓒ 2. tuition
3. to educate one's
4. to enter
5. qualification
6. to fulfil
Ⓓ Life-long learning
3 embarking on a career
4 has run/course
5 Assertiveness training
6 create; posts

...ings, you arrange them in a different way. (5)

...d your message before you .... it. (4)

...ur skills, you improve or refine them. (4)

...omeone or something, you notice them. (4)

...omeone's progress, you record their development over

...emic' in the sense of '..................... from practice'. (8)

10 If someone is .... , they have many different skills. (9)

Down

1 The .... sense of a word is its negative meaning. (10)

4 If you get .... to new ideas, you have the chance to experience them. (7)

5 If you connect the .... , you realise that something is related to something else. (4)

F Complete the webpage with the words from the box.

| choice | employers | feedback | graduates | role | skilled | ~~work~~ |

+ www.placementinfo.com

RateMyPlacement.co.uk

By creating a website that allows students to review work placements, Oliver Sidwell is leading an intern revolution and giving power to sometimes voiceless student employees.

Along with three friends from university, Oliver Sidwell set up RateMyPlacement.co.uk to help students find the right ......_work_.....[1] placements and internships. Placements are assessed through unique, detailed peer-to-peer ....[2], allowing previous interns to review the ....[3] so their successors can make better-informed choices. As well as guiding students and ....[4] to the best placements, the website encourages businesses to make their internships more rewarding and worthwhile (rather than leaving their new staff permanently stationed at the photocopier). The website is now a valuable resource for ....[5] and future employees alike, giving greater power and freedom of ....[6] to interns and providing a pool of ....[7] and motivated potential employees to recruiters.

TEXT AND GRAMMAR

A **Complete the text with the correct form of the verbs in brackets.**

'In-see-Ad?'
'No, I 've never heard [1] (never / hear) of it.'

Soon after I ....[2] (begin) the process of telling my family, friends, employer and even dentist that I ....[3] (leave) the US to move to Insead's Singapore campus and study on its MBA programme, I ....[4] (discover) that my acquaintances in the US ....[5] (tend) to be more provincial in their understanding of business schools.

In a few weeks from now, I ....[6] (leave) my home in small-town New Jersey, US, to join the Singapore cohort. How did I, a young professional born, raised and educated in the US,

make the decision to study for an international MBA?

I studied in North Carolina where I ....[7] (develop) a keen interest in international affairs. During my undergraduate years, I ....[8] (study) overseas in London. And later I ....[9] (accept) the opportunity to work in Waterloo, Belgium, the European headquarters for Johnson & Johnson, where I managed technology solutions for J&J's medical devices sector. I ....[10] (return) to the North American headquarters where I created a similar platform.

While I ....[11] (be) still in Belgium a senior manager had urged me to apply to Insead and I rapidly ....[12] (realise) that the school was the place where I could continue my development towards an international career.

The existence of Insead's Singapore campus ....[13] (make) the school that much more compelling because of my desire to have a global understanding of business which up until then ....[14] (only / include) North America and Europe.

B **Complete the sentences with suitable prepositions.**

1 After I left school with four 'A' levels, I went to do a degree ....in........ French with Business Studies .... York University.

2 You need to have passion .... what you do, as well as having a good understanding .... what's going on in the marketplace. This applies .... anything you want to do.

3 I've just finished studying .... a linguistics degree .... Madrid University.

4 Interns back home get paid .... average about 500 euros .... month.

5 As a result .... a downturn .... the economy, people are starting to spend less money .... branded consumer goods.

6 The company relies .... its sales force .... timely market information .... product sales, customer buying habits and competitor activity.

7 The Chinese appliance maker Haier has risen .... a nearly bankrupt collective enterprise 25 years ago .... one of the most successful companies in China.

8 Their approach enables managers to understand interactions .... various parts of the organisation and to spot opportunities .... productive collaboration.

9 Most staff members expressed interest .... participating .... various training programmes.

10 Very often, it is not just the sales staff that benefit .... customer awareness training.

C **Read the passage below about a company's view of mentoring.**

- In each of the spaces 1–10, one word has been removed.
- Write **one** suitable word for each space in the answer box below.

OUR VIEW OF MENTORING

An important element of developing our common future ....[1] the sharing of knowledge and experience, giving people the opportunity to learn from ....[2] other.

To support this approach we offer mentoring for the mutual benefit ....[3] our employees' personal development and the company ....[4] large.

For example, mentoring enables people facing major change – ....[5] as a global assignment – to get support and guidance from someone who ....[6] had previous experience. This helps our people.....................[7]

adapt more rapidly – and so be more effective in their new roles.....................[8] turn, mentors can learn something new about themselves and the organisation.

Our view of mentoring is that the mentor, as an experienced and respected individual, is able to reflect back constructively on a mentee's thoughts, ideas, feelings, behaviours and situations ....[9] that the mentee gains perspective and is challenged in their way of thinking and operating. It is ....[10] unique opportunity for both mentee and mentor to learn and grow.

Answer box		
1 ....is........	5	8 ....
2	6	9 ....
3	7	10 ....
4		

D **Read the passage below about performance appraisal.**

- In most of the lines 1–14 there is **one extra word** which does not fit. Some lines, however, are correct.
- If a line is **correct**, put a tick (✓) in the space provided.
- If there is an **extra word** in the line, write that word in the space provided.

For a performance appraisal to be an effective, the employee who is to be appraised	1 ....an..........
should be given advance notice of the performance appraisal interview and be informed	2 ....✓...........
of its purpose. In addition, it is useful to supply with an appraisal form to be completed	3 ....
and returned before the interview takes place. This should allow the employee for time	4 ....
to evaluate their performance as well as to identify any areas in which they would like	5 ....
either additional support and training. Another purpose of the appraisal form is to	6 ....
provide a structure for the interview. Very often, the employee is asked to reflect and on	7 ....
their job description to start off with and make the suggestions as to how it should be	8 ....
modified even if certain aspects of it are no longer appropriate. The employee is then	9 ....
invited to summarise their achievements and to comment on their strengths and	10 ....
weaknesses. Together with the supervisor, the employee can discuss about how to build	11 ....
on their strengths and also agree on a plan or to address any weaknesses identified.	12 ....
Finally, new objectives can be negotiated so as to enhance a motivation and ensure that	13 ....
the employee's work is geared towards the overall objectives of the company.	14 ....

A   **Write a report (200–250 words) to the Head of your HR Department.**

You recently attended an assertiveness training workshop organised by the department. The Head of HR has asked you to write a short report about the training.

In your report

- describe what you liked about the workshop and what you found useful

- mention one point that you did not like and explain

- describe one course or workshop you would like to attend in the future

- explain how this course or workshop would be useful to you and to the company.

Report on the Assertiveness Training Workshop

The aim of this report is to give my feedback on the two-day Staff Training & Development workshop I attended at our Headquarters on 26th and 27th January.

B   ◀» 4 **Listen to five different employees in a performance appraisal interview. Decide which of the supervisor's questions each employee is answering.**

- Write one letter (**a–e**) next to the number of the speaker.

- Do not use any letter more than once.

Speaker 1 ....

Speaker 2 ....

Speaker 3 ....

Speaker 4 ....

Speaker 5 ....

a) Is your job description up to date?

b) What have been your contributions, besides achieving your target, since your last performance appraisal?

c) Which of your previous appraisal objectives have you achieved?

d) Is there anything in your job that you have problems with?

e) Is there anything in your job you would say you could do better in the future?

C   ◀» 4 **Listen again and answer the questions.**

1   Who has a very varied job? Speaker .....

2   Who is not particularly happy with the way they organise their time? Speaker .....

3   Who is planning to do a training course? Speaker .....

4   Who is sometimes unfairly criticised? Speaker .....

5   Who would not like to have to write an official report regularly? Speaker .....

D ◀ 5 **Listen to how certain sounds are linked together in these sentences.**

1 We all_agree the previous course was_a lot_easier.

2 The information_I get_is_often_out_of date.

Explanation
When a word ends with a consonant sound and the word immediately after begins with a vowel sound, we usually link those two words.

◀ 5 **Listen again and practise the sentences.**

E ◀ 6 **Indicate where similar links could be made in these sentences. Then listen to check your answers.**

1 Let's talk about it in more detail.

2 Those courses are always intensive.

3 First of all, I just analyse the company's needs.

4 She's been acting as a coach for a company director.

5 A mentor is often someone who has a lot of experience.

◀ 6 **Listen again and practise the sentences.**

F ◀ 7 **We often have to check and correct information. When there is a mistake or a misunderstanding, we can use stress to put it right. Listen to these examples.**

1 A: So we all meet again on the 30th. Is that right?

   B: Sorry, no. Our next meeting is on the 13th.

2 A: Can I just check the first name, please? Is that F-R-A-N-C-I-S?

   B: C-E-S. F-R-A-N-C-E-S. Mrs Frances Potter.

G ◀ 8 **Underline the part which Speaker B will stress most to correct the misunderstandings in the following exchanges. Then listen to check your answers.**

1 A: Let me just check that. First, the Leadership Skills course starts next Tuesday.

   B: Not quite. It starts on Thursday.

2 A: ... and if I understood you correctly, the Leadership Skills course is free of charge.

   B: Sorry, no. It's the Computer Skills course that's free of charge.

3 A: Did you say the seminar room is on the first floor?

   B: No, it's on the third floor, actually.

4 A: The number of participants has now increased to 25.

   B: To 29! And we're expecting even more.

5 A: So you graduated from the University of Chester.

   B: Leicester, actually. I graduated from the University of Leicester in 2008.

6 A: ... and the freelance trainer is Jeremy Langford, L-A-N-G- ...

   B: Sorry, that's spelt L-A-N-K-F-O-R-D.

UNIT 3 Energy

A **Complete each set of sentences with the same word.**

1 In India and China, ...demand........ for oil is rising incredibly fast.
Instead of keeping huge numbers of books in stock, publishers now offer to print them on ...demand..........
Efficient project managers will always be in ...demand..........

2 Their proposal is definitely .... considering.
The person at the head of Exxon Mobil must be .... a fortune.
With the dollar in decline against the euro, profits in France and Germany were .... much more than those in the US.

3 Several companies have moved production to low-..................... sites in Central and Eastern Europe.
We deliver all our goods to your doorstep at no extra ....
Energy is probably the supermarket industry's number one operating ....
next to shelf stock.

4 The plant's production capacity will .... from eight to nine million tonnes next year.
Most western car manufacturers are hoping to .... into the new Chinese consumer market.
If we want to .... our business, we will need to borrow heavily.

5 Some countries have .... in for a lot of criticism for not signing the Kyoto accords.
There were signs that nuclear energy would soon .... back into favour.
A more in-depth study would .... up with some solutions.

B **Match the words 1–6 with the words a–f to make compounds.**

1 fuel-cell   a) turbines
2 wind   b) technology
3 solar   c) energies
4 carbon   d) panels
5 renewable   e) power
6 tidal   f) emissions

C **Complete the sentences with a compound from Exercise B.**

1 Intelligent Energy has raised £20m to finance commercialisation of its hydrogen
fuel-cell technology..., which has been used to power motorcycles, propeller aircraft and domestic boilers.

2 All countries should have international targets for reducing ....
....................., not just developing ones.

3 Bob Smith, Chief Executive of Pulse Tidal, says the UK is a good place to develop
...., having a long coastline that can boast some of the most powerful tidal streams in the world.

4 Clipper Windpower, a California-based renewable energy group, will develop several offshore ...., each capable of generating 7.5 megawatts of electricity.

5 A photovoltaic installation typically includes an array of ....
...................., an inverter, batteries and interconnection wiring.

6 Experts say that even though China is moving towards more ....
...................., coal will remain as a primary source of fuel for the foreseeable future.

D **Complete the sentences with the verbs from the box.**

> deny   stifle   curb   wean   move

1 Some experts argue that politically-driven support for particular technologies will .... innovation.

2 Planning to .... away quickly from hydrocarbons is unrealistic.

3 Mr Lund does not .... the science of climate change and says there is an 'urgent' need to respond to it.

4 Having been one of the first countries to impose a carbon tax, Norway has really managed to .... greenhouse gas emissions from its oil industry.

5 It probably won't be easy to .... the world off oil and gas because hydrocarbons are the energy source that our entire civilisation is built on.

E **Complete this text with words formed from the words given.**

efficient
promote

When the International Energy Agency last week cautioned that high oil prices could be here to stay and called for greater energy _efficiency_ [1] and the ....[2] of alternative energy sources, its warning had a decidedly 1970s feel.

speculate / stable

The IEA believes this new rise in oil prices does not merely reflect ....[3] trading activity and concerns about ....[4] in the Middle East but rather the fundamental balance of supply and demand. Rising global demand for oil has been driven by strong economic ....[5] in the US and China, while limited capacity in ....[6] and refining leaves the oil market vulnerable to shocks and price surges.

grow
produce

expand
expect

But, in contrast to the experience of the 1970s, the impact of $50 a barrel oil on global growth and inflation has been fairly limited. The rise in the oil price last year did damp growth but the ....[7] remains fairly healthy. While headline inflation rose last year, core inflationary pressures and, crucially, inflation ....[8] remain contained. Financial markets do not seem concerned that energy prices will spark higher inflation.

industry

credible
like

Adjusted for inflation, the oil price stands at only half the level of its 1970s peak. Past efforts at increasing energy efficiency also make ....[9] economies less vulnerable to an oil price surge. But another difference is the greater anti-inflation ....[10] of the world's leading central banks. The experience of last year has led to greater confidence that the 1970s provide a poor guide to ....[11] events this year.

strong
cycle

In the US, last year's concerns about the ....[12] of economic expansion have faded. Weaker ....[13] expansions in continental Europe and Japan, meanwhile, leave them more vulnerable to the effect on growth of higher oil prices. But few economists see the impact of oil prices as the most important factor in explaining weak ....[14] in these economies, which have struggled to promote domestic, demand-led growth.

perform

A The passage below is part of an article about nuclear power. Complete it with *a*, *an* or *the*. Write Ø where no article is necessary.

Nuclear power, once the target of protests and demonstrations, has been transformed into the unexpected darling of some sections of _the_ [1]green lobby.

............[2] reason is simple: ....[3] nuclear energy offers ....[4] hope of producing power on ....[5] large scale without burning ....[6] fossil fuels. That would solve what many regard as ....[7] biggest threat ....[8] planet faces: ....[9] global warming, caused by a dramatic rise in ....[10] level of carbon dioxide since ....[11] industrialisation.

As people still want ....[12] benefits of industrialisation and as developing countries pursue ....[13] economic development, some experts depict ....[14] once-maligned nuclear industry as the best solution.

The nuclear industry has itself assisted this transformation, through ....[15] development of new technologies designed to make nuclear power safer and to deal with ....[16] long-term problems such as the disposal of ....[17] waste.

B In the next part of the article, all six instances of the indefinite article have been removed. Insert the missing articles where they belong.

Ⱥ key question is whether nuclear energy would be economically viable. The upfront costs are discouragingly high at estimated $1,300 to $1,500 per kilowatt to build nuclear plant, which works out as roughly twice what it costs to build gas-fired power station. However, proponents claim that over the life of nuclear plant, it can generate energy at cost comparable to or even cheaper than that of conventional fossil-fuel power.

C Match the sentence halves.

1 A fall in the gas price might deter people

2 *All* countries should have international targets

3 In 2008, there was 155 billion dollars invested

4 People in developing countries have the same rights

5 Scientists are looking for ways to reduce our dependence

6 The inescapable truth seems to be that we need a substitute

7 What could reduce urban air pollution dramatically is a switch

a) for petrol.

b) for reducing carbon emissions, not just developing ones.

c) from fossil fuels to hydrogen.

d) from turning to renewable energy.

e) in clean energy worldwide.

f) on oil.

g) to basic energy as we have.

D Complete the article with suitable prepositions.

Companies bow to pressure on CO_2

More than 70 per cent of the FTSE 500 companies have agreed to help investors assess the impact they make on global climate change by disclosing the amount of carbon dioxide they produce.

The Carbon Disclosure Project, supported by a coalition __of__ [1] institutional investors with more than \$21,000bn ....[2] assets, wrote to every company in the index of the world's biggest companies, asking ....[3] information about their output of greenhouse gases. The companies were also asked whether they considered climate change a commercial risk or an opportunity, and to outline the risks.

James Cameron, chairman of the Carbon Disclosure Project, funded by a variety of charities, said investors should welcome the opportunity to know more ....[4] companies' risk from climate change: 'Nobody can be ....[5] greater disclosure and transparency,' he said, adding that the number of companies responding ....[6] the letter showed how the issue of climate change was rising up the corporate agenda. Investors could also benefit by understanding a company's output of greenhouse gases, which are coming ....[7] increasing regulation in many parts of the world. Countries that have ratified the United Nations brokered Kyoto protocol on climate change – the treaty came ....[8] force in 2005 – must reduce their emissions of greenhouse gases such as carbon dioxide, which cause climate change.

Businesses are expected to bear the brunt of these emissions cuts, as they account ....[9] the bulk of emissions in most places. In the US, which has rejected the Kyoto treaty, some states have been asking companies to reduce their greenhouse gas output ....[10] a voluntary basis. Paul Dickinson, coordinator of the Carbon Disclosure Project, said companies were likely to make a clean breast of their emissions in responding to the project's questions. 'They wouldn't want to lie ....[11] their investors.'

FT Publishing
FINANCIAL TIMES

E Read the passage below about oil and militarisation.

- In most of the lines 1–14 there is **one extra word** which does not fit. Some lines, however, are correct.
- If a line is **correct,** put a tick in the space provided.
- If there is an **extra word** in the line, write that word in the space provided.

As Europe and the US are becoming more dependent on imported oil, the use of military

personnel to protect vulnerable oil installations is bound to increase.

Because in the older industrialised countries have already used up most of their domestic 1 ......in......

oil reserves, most of the imported oil now comes from unstable countries in the developing 2 ......✓......

world, where vast, untapped oil reserves can still be found there. Many of those countries 3 ....

are ravaged by ethnic and religious conflicts, often aggravated by an inequitable 4 ....

distribution of oil revenues. This inequality gives rise to an opposition movements which 5 ....

are often crushed by the ruling elites, thus triggering a destructive spiral of violence. In 6 ....

addition too, as some of those emerging oil producers are former colonies, part of their 7 ....

population sees the Western involvement as a continuation of imperialism. 8 ....

Considering that oil is at the reason for such involvement, oil pipelines and refineries are 9 ....

seen as any legitimate targets by belligerent groups. In the past 50 years, the West has 10 ....

traditionally responded to this challenge by using his military means to guarantee the 11 ....

unhindered flow of oil. As both China and India are also building up their military 12 ....

capability to control over oil supplies from the Middle East, it is obvious that an alternative 13 ....

solution to the problem of a security needs to be worked out internationally. History has 14 ....

shown that excessive militarisation all too often leads to conflict.

A Complete the sentences with linkers from the box.

| given | however | in order to | thus | despite | ~~although~~ | unless |

1 *Although* there will be a big increase in CO_2 emissions in India, per capita emissions in developed countries will still be far higher than in India.

2 Garnex, the Belgian retailer, said it achieved a 3 per cent reduction in electricity usage last year from an annual energy budget of more than €5m, ... increasing its shop floor area.

3 Observers say Indian companies' aggressive bids in exploration auctions reflect a readiness to accept a lower rate of return than western companies .... secure a strategic asset.

4 Peter Morgan, economist at HSBC in Tokyo, believes the indirect impact of slower global growth – and .... lower demand for Japanese exports – is twice the direct impact in terms of reduction to GDP.

5 The world will soon experience a severe energy crunch .... the major energy firms stop digging ever deeper into existing reserves.

6 Today solar energy is one of the most popular alternative sources of energy. Ten years ago, ..., it was still widely regarded as impractical.

7 .... the extent of the climate change crisis, we all need to learn a radically new way of thinking.

B Write a report (maximum 150 words) on the chart below.

- The bar chart below shows the levels of a country's investment budget for the development of its railway and road infrastructure for the period 2006–2010 (in millions of euros).

- Use the information from the chart to summarise the changes in the transport infrastructure budget.

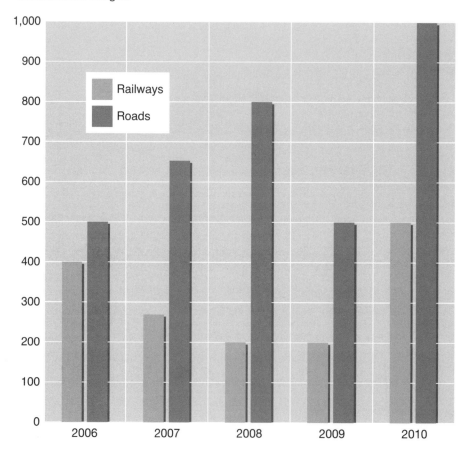

C ◄» 9 Listen and complete the notes below.

- You will hear a consultant giving a talk to a group of business managers about saving energy in the workplace.

- As you listen, complete the notes below using up to three words or a number.

Saving energy in the workplace

Lighting

Switch off the lights if there is .... [1] .

Careless use of artificial light costs companies ....
.... [2] every year.

Installing dimmers and motion sensors can be ....
.... [3] .

Heating

This also covers two closely related areas, i.e., ...
.... [4] .

In company buildings, ... [5] of the energy consumed is used for space conditioning.

If you want to extend the life of your equipment, ...
.... [6] is absolutely essential.

It is worth spending money on programmable thermostats because they are
.... [7] .

Office equipment

If you leave your office for more than .... [8] minutes, turn your computer off.

The computer monitor typically consumes .... [9] of the total energy used by the system.

Employees should be encouraged not to use the photocopier during
.... [10] .

Copiers often have automatic controls to reduce their power consumption during
.... [11] .

Such a copier can save you up to .... [12] in electricity compared to standard models.

D Before you listen, think of how these phrases from decision-making meetings could be completed.

Disagreeing indirectly

1 I'm not so .... I agree with you there.

2 I see things a little .... from you.

Emphasising a point

3 I .... think it's important to act quickly.

4 We .... can't afford to let the competition act first.

5 I know I keep .... on about this, but it's our reputation that's at stake.

Avoiding making decisions

6 Let's not .... any hasty decisions.

7 Let's .... our options open.

8 We should .... this through a bit more.

9 I'm in two .... about it really.

E ◄» 10 Now listen and complete the phrases with the words you hear.

Marketing

A **Complete the sentences with words and phrases from the box.**

catalogues   cold calling   door-to-door   e-mails   mailshots   ~~pop-up adverts~~
relationship management   social media   text messaging   word-of-mouth

1   Many people say they don't mind ..... *pop-up adverts* ...... on their favourite websites if it helps to keep them free.

2   Bulk advertising sent by post is known as ....

3   .... is a marketing method that consists in randomly phoning prospective customers.

4   Customer .... refers to the systems and processes that companies use to interact with customers.

5   .... selling used to work well for some products and services, such as vacuum cleaners and encyclopedias, but it has now fallen out of favour with many people.

6   Flicking through .... is often considered a thing of the past as most people now want to consult websites.

7   Some people believe that .... marketing via YouTube, Facebook and other social networking sites will soon replace print and television marketing.

8   The ever-growing number of mobile phone users has made .... a popular way to market to customers.

9   .... referrals is a powerful form of marketing that costs nothing: your customers do the marketing for you.

10 A lot of people aren't happy to receive .... about special promotions as they just clutter up the inbox.

B **Complete each set of sentences with the same word.**

1   Apparently, women control 72 per cent of purchasing and .... spending in the US.

   Many retailers and .... goods companies acknowledge that women are in charge of shopping and household spending.

   A glass .... is someone that companies can see through and know exactly how they behave and how they think.

2   Home Depot, the US home improvement retailer, has .... a range of home products by a female designer.

   Home2u successfully re- .... its marketing campaign.

   Our bank has .... a commercial insurance service for small businesses.

3   It seems that consumer companies, still predominantly .... by men, need to listen more to female customers.

   Barclays put effort into communicating specifically with women. For example, they sponsor 'Women In Business Awards' and .... marketing seminars.

   The company believes that the move will save it money in the long ....

4 These coats look like Armani, they feel like Armani, but they .... a fraction of the price.

With increased competition prices are pushed down, inviting more competitors such as supermarket low-..................... home brands.

Under Trilantic's ownership, MW Brands increased profits by about 50 per cent, partly due to .... savings from closing factories in France.

5 Market research shows that young Hispanic customers are an important .... group.

Some retail sectors which were considered traditionally 'male' are now beginning to .... female consumers.

What promotional events will you organise bearing in mind the .... market?

C Match the words 1–6 with the words a–f to make compounds.

1	consumer	a)	gap
2	viral	b)	spending
3	mass	c)	share
4	market	d)	marketing
5	customer	e)	market
6	earnings	f)	loyalty

D Complete the sentences with the compounds from Exercise C.

1 Retail sales growth has slowed and businesses fear that ...... *consumer* *spending* ..... will suffer this year as public sector jobs are cut and incomes squeezed.

2 The .... with men is expected to narrow further as the number of women being educated grows at a greater rate than the number of men being educated.

3 We sell these clothes to the .... in department stores and to high earners in boutiques.

4 As women tend to be less influenced by ads, subtler ways of communicating such as word-of-mouth marketing and .... might work.

5 Walmart introduced its MoneyCard largely to build .... among its primarily low-income core customers, many of whom lack bank accounts.

6 China now accounts for half of sales and all of operating profit, with a .... two-thirds bigger than HP and Dell combined.

E Cross out the word in each group which does not normally make a compound with the noun in bold.

1	**customer**	profile	loyalty	~~deficit~~	research
2	**advertising**	campaign	loan	budget	agency
3	**marketing**	trade	mix	intelligence	guru
4	**market**	study	venture	research	economy
5	**product**	endorsement	development	line	balance
6	**price**	promotion	account	tag	range
7	**brand**	image	name	production	awareness
8	**consumer**	expense	resistance	goods	behaviour

A Read the first part of a book review. Cross out the two incorrect options each time. (Ø means 'no pronoun'.)

Can marketing save the world?

Well, it can certainly try. In fact, it had better try, since people now invest more of their minds, hearts and spirits in their commercial lives.

They also have heightened expectations of business and its potential to improve the world, according to Philip Kotler, the S.C. Johnson & Son Professor of International Marketing, ~~which~~ / whose / ~~that~~[1] 47th book, *Marketing 3.0: From Products to Customers to the Human Spirit*, offers practitioners a framework for thriving in this emerging environment.

Kotler's book explores the changes *that / ∅ / who*[2] are cultivating a more enlightened sort of marketing, one *who / that / whose*[3] powers are being enlisted to help solve urgent problems.

Three forces — cheap computers and mobile phones, low-cost Internet access and open-source software — are driving this shift, Kotler writes, and have fostered a 'values-driven', networked world in *that / whom / which*[4] collaboration is easy and ubiquitous.

This 'new wave' technology also presents opportunities for marketers to engage consumers as individuals *whose / that / which*[5] needs extend beyond mere material goods — and as actors *who / ∅ / which*[6] want a bigger say in how and what a company produces, to ensure better outcomes for themselves and for society.

If 'Marketing 1.0' was a product-focused enterprise born of the Industrial Revolution and 'Marketing 2.0' was a customer-focused effort leveraging insights gained from information technology then, Kotler says, marketing's latest incarnation must do even more. It must engage people in ways *who / that / whose*[7] provide 'solutions to their anxieties to make the globalised world a better place.' Practitioners must, as never before, understand and respond to the values *that / ∅ / who*[8] drive customer choice.

B In the second part of the book review, the four relative pronouns are missing. Insert them where necessary.

And if, as Kotler argues, customers are the new brand owners, it's clear that their values will significantly influence those brands. Companies 'get' the 3.0 model, he says, will integrate the right values into every aspect of their business and then market that mission to their audience. 'The company wants to live out a set of values and these values give the company its personality and purpose', Kotler says.

Kotler even draws comparisons between Marketing 3.0 and the agenda outlined in the United Nations Millennium Development Goals of 2000, endorsed efforts to eradicate poverty and hunger, advance universal primary education and reduce child mortality. Profit will result when consumers appreciate a company's efforts to improve human well-being – whether that is The Walt Disney Company working to address wellness issues facing children or S.C. Johnson & Son's positioning as a sustainable family business serves millions of people living on less than $1 a day.

Marketing 3.0 is selling hope along with the soap, touching people's hearts and minds. It's a transformation, says Kotler, time has come.

C Complete these sentences using a relative clause with *that*.

1 (An expert designed their marketing campaign.)

Do you know the name of the expert ....*that designed*......their marketing campaign?

2 (Some products were withdrawn.)

Have we got a report on the products ....?

3 (Some people regard advertising as a waste of money.)

People .... as a waste of money shouldn't be working for our agency.

4 (A product launch was postponed.)

The product launch .... may never actually take place.

5 (We have two receptionists. One is fluent in Chinese.)

Do you know the one .... fluent in Chinese?

6 (Some documents were left on my desk.)

The documents .... on my desk were marked 'Confidential'.

7 (We launched an advertising campaign last month.)

The advertising campaign .... last month was very successful.

8 (They recalled some products.)

The products .... were a danger to public health.

9 (We hired three consultants last year.)

Linda Steiner is one of the consultants .... last year.

10 (Tim left some documents on his desk.)

The documents .... on his desk were all marked 'Confidential'.

11 (Marketing gurus write all sorts of things.)

Don't believe all the things .... write.

12 (I met someone at the Sales conference.)

Someone .... at the Sales conference gave me some excellent advice.

D Look at Exercise C. Indicate in which sentences *that* can be replaced with *which*, *who* and/or nothing (Ø).

Sentences 1 – 6 (*that* as subject)   **Sentences 7 – 12 (*that* as object)**

1 .....*who*.....   4 ....   7 ....   10 ....

2 ....   5 ....   8 ....   11 ....

3 ....   6 ....   9 ....   12 ....

E Complete these sentences with *when*, *where*, *whose* or *why*.

1 Professor Amir Sherifi? Is he the one ....*whose*..... book on marketing you recommended?

2 We could not think of any particular reason .... the campaign was so unsuccessful.

3 Zoe Revell is probably the only presenter .... talks I always enjoy.

4 Turkey is definitely the place .... we want to be sooner rather than later.

5 Do you remember the time .... door-to-door salesmen used to invade your living room?

6 They are renovating the premises .... we work.

A **Complete this extract from a presentation with the verbs from the box.**

ask	credit	cut	decided	increase	launched	plan
recognise	~~sounds~~	start	stopped	sum up		

So, to go back to what I was saying earlier, one of our objectives at Molrops Engineering was to reach a wider audience while at the same time reduce our advertising costs. That .... *sounds* .....[1] like a bit of a tall order, doesn't it? Maybe some of you are thinking, 'You can't have your cake and eat it'? Well, what I ....[2] to do in the next part of my presentation is precisely that: explain how we managed to ....[3] our advertising expenses by 12 per cent over the past two years and ....[4] sales by 5 per cent as a result of more effective marketing.

Let's ....[5] then with how we did it. As my grandmother used to say, the good things in life come in threes, so there we go: networking, referrals, blogs. Three words which summarise the future of advertising. First, we ....[6] paying our local radio extortionate fees for 30-second commercials and instead got involved with social networking sites like Twitter and Facebook. I can't tell you exactly how many new customers this move has brought into our business but an honest answer is: a lot more than we'd have dared to hope for two years ago.

Secondly, we ....[7] a word-of-mouth referral system with and for our employees: for each referral that an employee brings into our business, he or she gets a reward. This too has been working really well so far.

And thirdly, we also started our own blog and this is an ongoing experiment which is attracting more and more customers. Companies which doubt the effectiveness of blogs are probably those that think customers are naive and enjoy reading product-endorsing comments day in day out. But we ....[8] from the start that all comments on our blog would be genuine. We use our blog as a platform for communicating with our customers. That's what today's consumers want: dialogue, participation, trust. In fact, we can already ....[9] our blog with a sharp increase in revenues. But that's only part of the story. We've also invited our customers to tell us about the projects they're involved in, to tell us what would make their life and their work easier and all their ideas feed into the design and development of our next generation of products.

Let me just ....[10] you one question before I ....[11] the key points: what could be more satisfying for consumers than to ....[12] their input in the products they buy?

B **Look at the extract in Exercise A again. Prepare *one* PowerPoint slide with the key points.**

Remember the following points:

- title
- font size and colour
- bullet points instead of full sentences.

Use between 8 and 15 words.

C 🔊 11 **Listen to eight different presenters and decide which technique each one is using to make an impact.**

- Write one letter **(a–f)** next to the number of the speaker.
- You will need to use some of the letters twice.

Speaker 1 ....   a) using repetition

Speaker 2 ....   b) asking a 'real' or rhetorical question

Speaker 3 ....   c) quoting someone

Speaker 4 ....   d) emphasising key words or figures

Speaker 5 ....   e) building rapport with the audience

Speaker 6 ....   f) calling for action

Speaker 7 ....

Speaker 8 ....

D 🔊 12 **Listen to part of a presentation entitled** *New Technologies Are For Everyone***. Then answer the questions.**

1 Why are executives in their 30s and under at an advantage over older ones?

2 What are the new market segments mentioned by the presenter?

3 What is a new way in which unhappy customers interact with their brands?

4 Why might employers need to implement guidelines for staff use of social media?

5 Why do business schools have a vital role to play, according to the presenter?

E 🔊 12 **Listen again and complete the sentences with the words you hear.**

1 On the other hand, those in the 50s age group .... because they were exposed later in their careers to learning new technologies.

2 As a result, they may .... opportunities.

3 Executives who don't know how these mediums operate .... their clients' feedback because they can't see it in the first place.

4 Nor could they .... employee use of social media, which could .... employees misusing those media and causing marketing damage.

5 Without an .... of the .... of social media channels and new technology as marketing tools and .... , executives are ill-prepared for the 21st century.

F **Circle the word in each group which has a different stress pattern. Then check your answers in the Key.**

Example: business   channel   ⟨design⟩

> **Explanation**
>
> We say *business* and *channel* (stress on the first syllable) but *design* (stress on the second syllable).

1	guidelines	reward	feedback
2	decide	manage	respond
3	answer	occur	reduce
4	digital	genuine	effective
5	customer	revenues	consumer
6	referrals	expenses	company

🔊 13 **Listen and practise saying the words.**

UNIT 5 Employment trends

A **Complete the sentences with words from the box.**

| absenteeism | bonus | ~~casual~~ | migrant | portfolio |
| seasonal | security | self-employed | shift | turnover |

1 In summer, some students are employed as ...... *casual* ...... workers by our local hospital.

2 Apparently, all EU states have declined to ratify the UN Convention on the Rights of .... Workers and their Families.

3 Are you employed by a company or are you .... ?

4 In call centres, absence rates can be as high as 30 per cent and employee .... rates can be as high as 100 per cent.

5 In many countries, ... work is often available on farms and in orchards, vineyards and forests.

6 It is often said that .... work can have a very damaging effect on your sleep patterns.

7 Most people want to be paid reasonably and to be given some job .... and a degree of responsibility for their work.

8 The most common causes of .... are reported as headaches and migraine, colds and flu, back problems and stress.

9 Growing numbers of professionals are reinventing themselves by setting up as .... workers in a new employment phenomenon dubbed Giganomics.

10 If you do not meet your performance targets, you will lose your ....

B **Complete the pairs of synonyms with items from the box.**

| dismiss | lay off | leave | select | take on | ~~terminate~~ |

1 to end / ... *terminate* ... a contract

2 to fire / .... an employee

3 to recruit / .... staff

4 to make staff redundant / to .... staff

5 to choose / .... a candidate

6 to quit / .... one's job

C **Match the words 1–8 with the words a–h to make compounds.**

1	job	a)	skills
2	work-life	b)	package
3	attrition	c)	satisfaction
4	maternity	d)	security
5	redundancy	e)	rates
6	human	f)	leave
7	job	g)	resources
8	communication	h)	balance

D **Complete the sentences with compounds from Exercise C.**

1 Promotion opportunities, a friendly working atmosphere and flexible working hours are all factors which can affect ....*job*.... .....*satisfaction*.......

2 It doesn't matter how many hours you work: if you have worked continuously for the same employer for two years, you are entitled to have a ....
.... when you are laid off.

3 Despite high ...., call centres in India are expected to continue to grow.

4 Most employers today are looking for people who can work across a wide variety of tasks within the workplace so ...., the ability to get on with other people and work in a team, are particularly important.

5 High employee turnover is a huge challenge for ....
managers.

6 .... used to be a given, but today growing numbers of professionals are reinventing themselves by setting up as portfolio workers.

7 When my .... was up, my employers agreed to let me finish at 3 o'clock instead of 5 so I could spend more time with my baby.

8 Portfolio workers should be able to have a better ....
but the people who employ them often expect them to be on call 24/7.

E **Complete each set of sentences with the same word.**

1 The new regulations ...*apply*... to all companies employing 150 people or more.

Fraudsters can use your personal details to ...*apply*... for credit cards, loans and other financial products.

She is planning to ...*apply*... for a full-time job as a computer technician.

2 Our consultant helped us to resolve the conflict and to .... mutually beneficial relationships.

The new manager's ambition is to .... up the company to be an industry leader.

We will .... on last year's success and improve our earnings before interest and tax by 15 per cent.

3 How can consultation exist when company directors may be thinking of substituting their permanent workforce with a cheaper .... supply based overseas?

At the meeting, workers will vote whether to withdraw their .... or to continue working.

The company is desperately trying to keep .... costs down.

4 The manager soon .... a reputation as an expert on conflict resolution.

She worked extremely hard but .... only a meagre wage.

While he was in Canada, he .... a living as a music teacher.

5 The British car industry had one of its most depressing years on ....

The company was trying to raise production to a .... level.

The candidate should have a proven .... of excellent research or be able to demonstrate potential for such research.

6 Organisations are .... rid of staff but they will buy back some of them on a portfolio basis.

After I had the baby it was .... to be impossible to combine full-time work with my family commitments.

The work was .... too stressful and I started having trouble sleeping.

TEXT AND GRAMMAR

A **Complete the sentences with the *-ing* form or the infinitive of the verb in brackets.**

1   When you are a portfolio worker, your employers sometimes expect you ......*to be*.....
    (*be*) on call at all times.

2   People who work for a variety of employers sometimes find it hard ....
    (*say*) 'no' when they are asked to take on more work.

3   A lot of parents can't afford .... (*give up*) .... (*work*) full time
    to look after their children.

4   If you wish .... (*find*) a job in Human Resources, you should consider
    .... (*do*) a course in communication skills to begin with.

5   Jeff seemed .... (*be*) suffering from depression and was contemplating
    .... (*hand in*) his resignation.

6   If we fail .... (*meet*) our performance targets, we risk ....
    (*lose*) the bonus.

7   I don't mind .... (*do*) bits and pieces for a while but I intend
    .... (*go back*) to full-time work as soon as I can.

8   Emoticons may seem silly to some but sometimes they really help ....
    (*express*) the tone that you want.

B **Complete the text with some of the sentences a–h on page 31. You will only need six of the eight sentences.**

The puzzle of the lost women

Sari Baldauf did it at Nokia, Brenda Barnes at PepsiCo and Penny Hughes at Coca-Cola ....*f*....¹.

They are the headline-grabbing tip of an iceberg. Women graduates enter many companies and professional firms in nearly equal numbers to men but they drop out as they rise up the ranks. How to hold on to this talent and increase women's representation in senior jobs has become a serious concern.

Is discrimination to blame? ....² Or are women less ambitious, less willing to play power games and more susceptible to demands outside work?

All of these elements play a part, as several new studies reveal. A recent survey shows that 58 per cent of highly qualified women in the US have non-linear careers, spending part of them in jobs with reduced hours or responsibility, for example. Nearly four in ten take a complete break from work averaging just over two years.

For companies that lose talented women, the survey contains worrying news. None of those who left jobs in business, banking or finance wanted to return to their former employer. ....³

In career terms, stepping off the corporate treadmill is no bad thing for some high-fliers. Ms Barnes rose to the top of PepsiCo North America in her 22-year career there and then spent the best part of seven years with her children, while taking some directorships. ....⁴

Meanwhile Ms Hughes, who was president of Coca-Cola in Britain and Ireland before taking time out for her family, now holds prestigious non-executive directorships at companies including Gap, Reuters and Vodafone.

...............⁵ Even highly qualified women can have difficulty finding a job commensurate with their skills or getting any work at all after taking a break. The US survey demonstrates unequivocally that these women do not lose interest in their careers but they do lose out financially. ....⁶

This is partly because many choose to return to more flexible work. Those who opt for reduced hours can end up being sidelined. But it does not have to be this way. Jobs involving reduced hours can benefit employee and employer provided both are committed and can be flexible.

FT Publishing
FINANCIAL TIMES

a) None of this means women are necessarily less effective leaders.

b) Those who take a break from business and finance forfeit on average 28 per cent of their earning power.

c) In fact, the overriding factor in their decision to take a career break was not family, as people might assume, but lack of job satisfaction.

d) Is corporate culture at fault by favouring the linear career path traditionally taken by men?

e) Last month, she became chief executive of Sara Lee, the consumer goods company she joined only last year.

f) All three women quit top jobs at the height of their careers to pursue outside interests and responsibilities.

g) Equally, women must learn to manage their careers more effectively.

h) But such cases are unusual.

C **Read the passage below about job satisfaction.**

- In most of the lines **1–15** there is one **extra word** which does not fit. Some lines, however, are correct.

- If a line is **correct**, put a tick in the space provided.

- If there is an **extra word** in the line, write that word in the space provided.

According to a recent survey, most employees enjoy their work. Why then do so many	1 ......✓........
become sick of their jobs? The answer, according to the same survey, is that a poor	2 ....a........
management often erodes in one or all of the three underlying factors that underpin job	3 ....
satisfaction: achievement, fair of treatment and social acceptance among workmates.	4 ....
Such apparently simple needs are not easy to fulfil. Too many managers have a	5 ....
tendency to wreck under the natural enthusiasm of employees for their work. Most	6 ....
people enter in a new organisation and job with enthusiasm, eager to contribute, to feel	7 ....
proud of their work and their organisation. But perversely, many managers then appear	8 ....
to do their best to demotivate employees. In order to enjoy in a sense of achievement,	9 ....
an employee not only needs many meaningful and challenging work and pride in the	10 ....
company, but also recognition for a job they well done. A simple 'thank you' can	11 ....
influence no perceptions that the work is valued. However, only half of employees	12 ....
claim to have sufficient feedback and then if much of it tends to be negative.	13 ....
Constructive feedback is all too rare, probably because giving effective feedback on an	14 ....
employee's performance is one of the tasks that managers find most difficult.	15 ....

SKILLS AND PRONUNCIATION

A **Match the sentence halves.**

1 **Despite** not being paid particularly well,

2 There is still a large gender pay gap in the UK,

3 **In spite of** the sudden increase in orders,

4 He had excellent communication skills

5 **Although** he had been hired by the company time and again,

6 He was not even shortlisted for interview

7 **Even though** she had left her career for only one year,

8 None of them was awarded a bonus

a) **although** it has narrowed recently to about 16 per cent.

b) she incurred a heavy financial penalty when she returned to work.

c) **even though** they all had exceeded their sales targets.

d) they never offered him a permanent contract.

e) **in spite of** his excellent qualifications and considerable experience.

f) they did not take on more staff.

g) she never considered looking for another job.

h) **despite** his apparent shyness.

B **Complete the information with words from the box.**

stronger   of   noun   contrast   verb

• All the linkers in **bold** in Exercise A are used to express .... [1].

• *In spite of* and *despite* are followed by a .... [2] or noun phrase or a gerund.

• *Although* and *even though* are followed by a subject + ... [3] + complement.

• *Despite* is never followed by .... [4].

• *Even though* means the same as *although* but expresses a .... [5] contrast.

C **Express the ideas in two different ways, using linkers from Exercise A.**

1 Attrition rates are high. Call centres are expected to grow.
   Even though attrition rates are high, call centres are expected to grow.
   Despite high attrition rates, call centres are expected to grow.

2 Staff morale is relatively good. They have to deal with a lot of abusive calls.

3 He had been promised promotion. He decided to hand in his notice.

4 Working conditions were appalling. Employee loyalty was good.

5 The company has a formal grievance procedure. Staff hardly ever voice their complaints.

6 They were both quite flexible. They failed to find a mutually acceptable solution.

> **Tip**
> Whether you write a report, a letter or an e-mail, variety of sentence structure is one of the factors that make your writing more interesting and effective.

D Write a report (maximum 200 words) on the graphs below.

- The graphs illustrate employment trends in the manufacturing and service industry in a country and its capital city.
- Using the information from the graphs, write a report describing the general movements of employment levels in the period 2004–2010.

E ◀))) 14 Look at the graphs in Exercise D and listen to a presenter describing them. How many errors can you spot in the presentation?

◀))) 15 Listen and check your answers.

F Circle the word in each group which has a different stress pattern. Then check your answers in the Key.

Example: seasonal (employment) temporary

Explanation

We say *seasonal* and *temporary* (stress on the first syllable) but *employment* (stress on the second syllable).

1	permanent	flexible	abusive
2	attrition	promotion	atmosphere
3	security	economy	motivation
4	location	company	loyalty

◀))) 16 Listen and practise saying the words.

Ethics

A **Complete the definitions with words from the box.**

> accountability ~~Fairtrade~~ fraudulent nepotism sustainability
> supply chain stakeholders wrongdoing whistleblower

1 *Fairtrade* is a trading partnership based on dialogue, transparency and respect that seeks greater equity in international trade.

2 .... is the fact of being responsible for one's actions and ready to explain them if required.

3 .... methods or actions intend to deceive people, often in order to gain money illegally.

4 .... is the quality of being strong enough to continue existing or happening for a long time.

5 A..................... is someone who informs the public that the company they work for has engaged in illegal practices.

6 The .... is the series of people or organisations that are involved in passing products from the manufacturers to the public.

7 The .... are the people who are considered to be an important part of an organisation or society because they have responsibility within it and receive advantages from it.

8 .... is the practice of giving jobs to members of your family when you are in a position of power.

9 .... is illegal or immoral behaviour.

B **Complete the sentences with words from Exercise A.**

1 There is increasing demand for chocolate that is produced and sold through .... agreements, particularly in Europe.

2 .... reports are standard practice nowadays but a business can always find ways to hide illegal activities.

3 People who make .... insurance claims are liable to prosecution.

4 The manager choosing his nephew as deputy was a clear case of.....................

5 About a decade ago, ..., that is to say people who have an interest in how companies are run, started talking about corporate responsibility.

C **Write the opposite of the following adjectives.**

1 fair *unfair*
2 legal ....
3 moral ....
4 honest ....
5 convincing ....
6 responsible ....
7 ethical ....
8 prudent ....
9 accountable ....
10 direct ....

D Complete the word(s) in each sentence by writing in the missing letters. Each word is a compound or derivative of the word *law*.

1 She filed a l_ws_it against her former employer.

2 It seems a l_g_t_m_t_ expectation to know where your bank invests your money.

3 Although the money had been collected _ll_g_ll_, the committee l_g_l_s_d the funds and used them to pay off debts.

4 It turned out that the chemical had been l_wf_ll_ produced in a European country.

5 In Britain, a barrister is a l_wy_r who can argue cases in the higher courts of law.

6 Some people argue that nothing can l_g_t_m_s_ the use of children in advertising.

E Complete this text with words formed from the words given.

In March 2005, the sacking of Boeing's chief executive over an office affair raised many questions, not least whether it heralded a new era of corporate policing of executives' personal morals.

sure   Could snooping on workplace liaisons become part of the job of the ethics officer, whose role is to ....*ensure*....[1] that a company's code of conduct is understood and followed by every member of staff?

effect
employ
guide   'The dynamics of taking on a police function would fundamentally change the ....[2] of the ethics officer,' says Ms Gretchen Winter, an expert on professional responsibility. 'I think ....[3] might be less willing to come forward. The role of a neutral party to whom they can come for ....[4] might be compromised.'

judge   The ethics officer's job was thrown into sharp relief by the Boeing affair, in which the chief executive was ousted for behaviour that the company decided had 'reflected poorly' on his ....[5].

investigate   Ms Winter says the case provoked hot debate about where the line should be drawn. 'Some ethics officers used the Boeing case to talk about the ....[6] process, their relationship with boards, who the decision-makers are and how you handle issues of judgement versus violations of your code – or are they one and the same?' she says. 'What it did was illustrate the type of situation that ethics officers are called on to deal with every day – what kind of investigative process do you use, how do you determine

discipline / violate   appropriate ....[7] action if you find a ....[8], and who should be disciplined?'

The ethics officer draws up standards, provides a safe conduit for whistleblowers, investigates allegations and presents findings to a 'decision-maker' – typically the manager of the individual being investigated, she says.

relate   Ms Winter points out that there are CEOs who have had ....[9] at work and have remained in office. 'It's not the ethics officer's role to determine whether that
accept   behaviour is ....[10] or not,' she insists. 'That responsibility belongs to whoever employs the individual.'

press   The case came at a time when ....[11] was mounting on companies to take
comply   ethics more seriously – and on the professionals charged with ensuring ....[12].

grow   Why, given the rapid ....[13] in the number of ethics officers, are ethical lapses still so frequent in companies? It is partly that the ethics profession is young and also that it is far harder to change behaviour than simply to write and publish a code of conduct, Ms Winter replies.

A **Complete the sentences with the most appropriate modal verbs (positive or negative). An explanation is given in brackets.**

1 Only Peter or Sandra could have found this highly classified report. It .....*can't*..... have been Peter because he was on paternity leave. (*impossibility*) So it .... have been Sandra. (*logical conclusion*)

2 Why did you ring in sick? You weren't ill! You .... have rung in sick. (*criticism*)

3 One of our suppliers gave me a Rolex. I .... have declined such an expensive present. Now my colleagues think I take bribes. (*regret*)

4 I .... normally have accepted a post with a company that has such a poor environmental record but at the time I badly needed a job. (*if I hadn't needed a job* ...)

5 You .... have gone to Martin Weil's presentation on corporate responsibility. It was brilliant! Why weren't you there? (*it was recommended*)

6 What a pity you got up so early! We are not starting until 10.30. You .... have got up so early. (*it wasn't necessary*)

7 'Andrew didn't even say "hello" at the conference yesterday.'

'Well, he .... have seen you.' (*there's a possibility that he didn't see you*)

8 Why aren't they here yet? They .... have arrived hours ago. (*something expected didn't happen*)

B **Choose the best way to complete the exchanges below.**

1 A: I'm really disappointed that you didn't report those irregularities sooner.

B: Well, when do you think I .... *c* .... have reported them?

a) must **b)** may **c)** should

2 A: I can't find Liz anywhere.

B: Her coat's still here, so she .... have left the office early.

a) must **b)** can't **c)** would

3 A: The boss was furious. Next time I won't say anything.

B: Yeah, I think that's best. You .... have lost your job!

a) might **b)** can **c)** must

4 A: The report is very positive.

B: I agree. But on some criteria, like 'product information', we .... have done better.

a) would **b)** could **c)** might not

5 A: Last spring, they made 150 workers redundant.

B: I know. It .... have been a very difficult period for the automobile industry.

a) must **b)** should **c)** can

6 A: Where's Laurent?

B: I don't know. His PC is off, so he .... have gone home early today.

a) would **b)** shouldn't **c)** might

C **Complete the second sentence in each pair so that it has approximately the same meaning as the first sentence. Use between *two* and *five* words, including the word given.**

1 The public often ask companies not to hide their stance on environmental issues.　(**reveal**)

Companies *are often requested to reveal* their stance on environmental issues.

2 CEOs may sound very enthusiastic in their reports but you should always insist on hard evidence.　(**how**)

No .... CEOs may sound in their reports, you should always insist on hard evidence.

3 If we do not set up a corporate responsibility team, shareholders may lose confidence in our approach.　(**unless**)

Shareholders may lose confidence in our approach .... a corporate responsibility team.

4 Our company's safety record is substantially better than our competitors'.　(**nearly**)

Our competitors' safety record is .... ours.

5 We made a bad mistake when we said our suppliers were responsible for the delay in production.　(**blame**)

It was wrong of us .... the delay in production.

6 Our organisation has made every effort to get rid of age and gender discrimination.　(**stamp**)

Our organisation has made every effort .... age and gender discrimination.

7 If the CEO had not admitted wrongdoing at the last minute, our manager would have come under suspicion.　(**admitting**)

But .... wrongdoing at the last minute, our manager would have come under suspicion.

8 One of the directors pointed out to the board a number of inconsistencies in the report.　(**drew**)

One of the directors .... a number of inconsistencies in the report.

9 My boss was too impatient to read the report to the end.　(**that**)

My boss was .... not read the report to the end.

10 I think it would be a good idea if we listened more to what anti-globalisation movements have to say.　(**suggest**)

I .... listen more to what anti-globalisation movements have to say.

11 We are really excited about the conference.　(**forward**)

We .... the conference.

A **Write a report (200–250 words) to your Managing Director.**

You work for a new international organisation which is expanding rapidly. Your Managing Director has asked you to comment on the desirability of a Code of Conduct for all the staff in the future. Write a report in which you

- explain the usefulness / necessity of such a Code of Conduct

- explain how it would benefit both the organisation and its staff

- outline possible areas of content.

> ### Report on future Code of Conduct
>
> Ms Stella Hubert, Managing Director of our Berlin office, has requested this report on the desirability of a Code of Conduct for all our employees.
>
> The aim

B 🔊 17 **Listen to eight different people chairing meetings and decide what each one is doing.**

- Write one letter **(a–f)** next to the number of the speaker.

- You will have to use some letters twice.

Speaker 1 ....   a) opening the meeting

Speaker 2 ....   b) stating the purpose of the meeting

Speaker 3 ....   c) asking for clarification

Speaker 4 ....   d) calling on a speaker

Speaker 5 ....   e) interrupting a speaker

Speaker 6 ....   f) summarising decisions taken

Speaker 7 ....

Speaker 8 ....

C ◀)) **18 Listen to part of a radio interview with Goran Tielsen about socially responsible investment. Choose the best option, a), b), or c), to complete these sentences.**

1 Socially responsible investors …
 a) invest some of their money in environmental agencies and social institutions.
 b) make society generally more responsible.
 c) expect the companies they invest in to share the same moral values.

2 The Forum for Socially Responsible Investment is made up essentially of …
 a) forward-looking businesses.
 b) old age pensioners who want a better pension scheme.
 c) people who pay money into a pension fund or a bank account.

3 A majority of pension funds were found …
 a) to be to some extent ethical investors.
 b) to invest some of their money in arms-exporting companies.
 c) to have a tobacco company in their portfolio.

4 The forum sometimes encourages its members to …
 a) try and influence the activities of certain pension funds.
 b) boycott unethical high street banks and pension funds.
 c) stop investing in the tobacco and arms industries.

5 The forum is particularly proud of having …
 a) introduced the concept of ethical banking.
 b) made the idea of ethical banking very popular.
 c) done extensive research on ethical banks.

6 On the basis of the forum's recommendations, a number of banks …
 a) took steps to modify their lending policies.
 b) started investing more in environmental projects.
 c) lost their reputation as ethical investors.

7 The Third World debt has been …
 a) completely written off by high street banks everywhere.
 b) in large part transferred to official creditors.
 c) at the centre of a crisis since 1980.

8 Some countries might have improved their human rights record more quickly if …
 a) investors had boycotted them more effectively.
 b) more foreign companies had invested there.
 c) fewer companies had tacitly supported repression.

D ◀)) **19 Listen to how these modal perfects are pronounced. Then listen again and practise saying the sentences.**

1 It could've been worse. /ˈkʊdəv/
2 He must've been delayed. /ˈmʌstəv/
3 She can't have lost it. /ˈkɑːntəv/
4 They wouldn't have done it. /ˈwʊdəntəv/
5 I might've hit him! /ˈmaɪtəv/
6 You should've told me. /ˈʃʊdəv/

A **Complete each sentence with the best word. Use a good dictionary to help you if necessary.**

1 A .... *a* .... bank supports projects which deliver a positive impact socially and environmentally.

   a) sustainable   **b)** convertible   **c)** renewable

2 Business activities that take place unofficially, especially in order to avoid paying tax, constitute what we call the .... economy.

   a) grey   **b)** white   **c)** black

3 Continuing strong sales and earnings gains enabled the company to increase its shareholders' total .... on investment.

   a) dividend   **b)** return   **c)** bonus

4 Last year, ... debts caused by the recession wiped out the bank's operating profit.

   a) bad   **b)** gross   **c)** peak

5 Customers began withdrawing deposits, causing difficulties for the .... of the bank.

   a) liquidity   **b)** transparency   **c)** credibility

6 The company eventually went ...., leaving debts of £9 million.

   a) crash   **b)** bust   **c)** curtain

7 Are you interested in taking an active role in the business or would you rather be a .... partner?

   a) rampant   **b)** gravy   **c)** sleeping

8 The global crisis has clearly left many bank customers financially ....

   a) prevented   **b)** exposed   **c)** suspected

9 Incredible though it may seem, banks have no systems in place for managing their own cash ....

   a) debit   **b)** flow   **c)** subsidy

10 The money will be .... into your account on the 25th of the month.

   a) deposited   **b)** versed   **c)** reckoned

11 The Pakistani government has welcomed the approval of a $500m .... -free loan from the World Bank's International Development Association.

   a) charge   **b)** rate   **c)** interest

12 Dividends are paid to .... each year if adequate profits are made.

   a) customers   **b)** debtors   **c)** shareholders

13 The value of a company's shares is called ....

   a) equity   **b)** dividend   **c)** holding

14 The interest .... on the loan was 15 per cent.

   a) fee   **b)** rate   **c)** charge

15 We want to find a partner who will take a .... in our business.

   a) risk   **b)** stake   **c)** share

B **Match the verbs 1–7 with the nouns a–g to make common collocations.**

1 to open — a) a new client
2 to go b) outside the box
3 to take on c) one's portfolio
4 to diversify — d) an account
5 to spread e) bankrupt
6 to think f) a press statement
7 to issue g) a risk

C **Match the words 1–8 with the words a–h to make compounds.**

1 venture a) account
2 savings b) fund
3 debt c) evasion
4 bridging d) funding
5 overdraft e) angel
6 tax f) loan
7 pension g) facilities
8 business h) capitalist

D **Complete the sentences with compounds from Exercise C.**

1 A ..*venture   capitalist*.. is a speculator who makes money available for innovative projects.

2 A .... is just for a short period of time while longer-term financing is arranged.

3 He pleaded guilty to charges of bank fraud and ....

4 In terms of return, as a provider of .... , the return for us is merely the interest that we are paid on the loan.

5 It seems that most bank customers' use of .... is unintentional in nature.

6 A .... is a private investor who finances very small or start-up companies and may provide them with the benefit of his or her expertise.

7 A large number of .... s which invest a certain percentage ethically may still have in their main portfolio a tobacco or an arms-exporting company.

8 The average .... pays interest of less than 1 per cent and very few accounts offer a real return to savers after inflation and tax.

E **Complete this extract from a newspaper article with the words from the box.**

advisers   consumers   erosion   ~~expenses~~   proportion   savings

Almost a third of UK adults are falling back on their savings and investments to supplement their income.

Research published by Schroders has revealed that 31 per cent of Britons spent an average of £4,600 over the last 12 months to 'top up' their living ...*expenses*...[1].

A poll by Moneysupermarket.com, the comparison website, also found that over half of ....[2] said they have dipped into their ....[3] pots.

'The amount of capital being drawn down suggests that it is not just rainy day funds that are being drained but a significant ....[4] of individuals' long-term savings,' said Robin Stoakley of Schroders UK Intermediary Business.

The findings reveal that 55 per cent of financial ....[5] say their clients have suffered from capital ....[6] in the past 12 months.

FT Publishing
FINANCIAL TIMES

WORD POWER

A **Complete each set of sentences with the same multi-word verb from the box. Use the appropriate form of the verb each time.**

> give away   take off   bring down   turn down   get away

1 a) The whole banking system was .... not because risk management was deficient nor because greed was rampant but because bankers could not count.

  b) The government hopes these measures will help to .... inflation.

  c) They were threatening to .... the government by withdrawing from the ruling coalition.

2 a) The meeting dragged on and I didn't .... until seven.

  b) The charge was reduced to manslaughter and he .... with three years in prison.

  c) How did the shareholders let the banks .... with such folly?

3 a) Not only has the banking industry been spending money that is no longer there, it has been .... money that it only imagined it had in the first place.

  b) We have 1,000 CDs to .... to our readers.

  c) Phil tried to smile but his voice .... him ....

4 a) Jack was not doing very well so he became jealous when Mimi's career started ....

  b) I felt quite excited as the plane .... from Heathrow.

  c) It was so hot that I wanted to .... my shirt ....

5 a) It was a generous offer but he .... it ....

  b) Can you .... the TV .... ? I'm trying to work.

  c) Who would .... an invitation to go to Auckland?

B **Complete each sentence with the best word.**

1 We are giving .... b .... a free diary with tomorrow's newspaper.

  a) out   b) away   c) off

2 All business people know that you can carry .... for a while if you make no profits but not for very long.

  a) on   b) over   c) up

3 If you're in business and you .... out of cash, you're finished.

  a) fall   b) get   c) run

4 Our principal responsibility is to .... down the level of unemployment.

  a) bring   b) turn   c) take

5 Some people break the law and get away .... it.

  a) about   b) over   c) with

6 Last year the CEO .... out on a new sports car.

  a) flashed   b) splashed   c) trashed

7 We're all very happy that Sue's business has taken ....

  a) up   b) over   c) off

8 Any industry that pays .... in cash colossal profits that are largely imaginary will go bust quickly.

  a) out   b) up   c) over

C Complete the text with the verbs from the box.

announced	achieved	are	follows	grown	has improved
have improved	is being implemented	made	will be		

BENTIX INTERNATIONAL
Results Update

Bentix, the Luxemburg-based multi-brand health and personal care product manufacturer, ...announced...[1] today that its profits for the half year to 1 July ....[2] ahead of its expectations. This ....[3] a very strong performance by Pharma Vita, its over-the-counter health product operation, in February and March.

Chairwoman Helen Dejong said, 'We ....[4] very pleased with the performance of Pharma Vita. Since Spring last year, we have delivered two improved seasons, which, together with several other exciting initiatives, demonstrate how successfully our strategy ....[5].

Over the past eighteen months, the management ....[6] the efficiency of the business, ...[7] marketing more effective, ...[8] online sales significantly and ....[9] savings in production and advertising. These actions ....[10] operating margins.

However, it is not possible to say at this stage whether the second half will show the same level of profit growth.'

Bentix will now announce its interim results on Friday, 29 July.

D Six instances of the definite article, *the*, are missing. Insert them where they belong.

Our strategy for Bentix is to position brand as a major player in medium cost health and personal care arena, by not only expanding its antiseptics offering, but also diversifying into other health care products. Earlier this year we started testing essential oils and herbal remedies with some success and we will look to introduce more new product concepts over next 12 to 18 months. We will be deploying many of successful initiatives tested in first half before festive season.

A **Write a report (maximum 150 words) on the chart below.**

- The bar chart below shows the approximate levels of banking concentration in five different countries over a period of ten years.
- Use the information from the chart to summarise the changes in banking concentration.

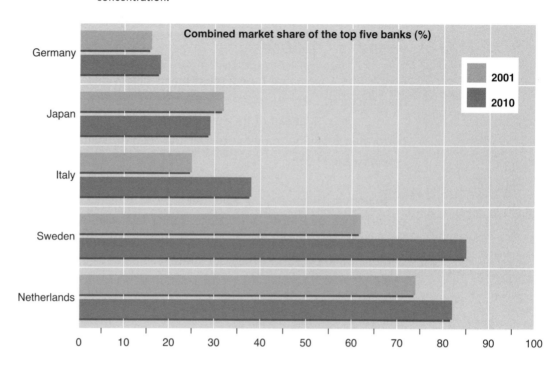

B ◀» 20 **Listen and complete the Chairman's statement.**

I am delighted to present my third report to shareholders as Chairman of Castel International following another year of strong performance.

Our company has consistently delivered superior total shareholder ....[1] since its creation in 1989.

The results of the company were very strong and at the top end of the industry peer group. Net ....[2] rose by 9 per cent while net ....[3] rose by 22 per cent to €658m.

In May, the company announced its intention to return ....[4] cash to shareholders through a progressive ....[5] policy and a rolling share ....[6] programme. Both of these have been initiated. The ....[7] dividend was increased by 8 per cent and the directors propose that the ....[8] dividend be increased by 7 per cent giving a total for the year of 40 cents a share, an overall increase of 12 per cent.

This dividend, if ....[9] at the Annual General Meeting, will be paid on 30th March next year to shareholders on the register on 15th January.

At the same time, the company has begun its rolling share buyback programme and had already ....[10] 2 million shares by the year end. It is the company's intention to proceed with this programme through next year.

C ◀)) 21 **Listen to the first part of a radio programme. Decide if the following statements are true (T) or false (F).**

1 According to Tricia Ashcroft, it is utterly impossible for a small business to raise finance when there is a recession.

2 Tricia does not believe that the economy has fully recovered.

3 Despite the crisis, having a great business idea is often enough for a new entrepreneur to get a loan.

4 Tricia argues that Bob Hope's quote does to some extent reflect the reality of banking.

5 When entrepreneurs ask for a loan, banks tend to demand that they have capital to secure the loan.

6 Tricia says that all banks are reluctant to support innovative projects.

7 Triodos specialises in supporting scientific and artistic projects.

D ◀)) 22 **Listen to the second part of the radio programme and answer the questions.**

1 Why is it particularly difficult for new clean tech companies to access finance?

2 What makes the Bowens' product 'green'?

3 How did they try to raise capital in the first year?

4 What sources of capital have they had access to since 2006?

5 What is Logicor's mission?

E ◀)) 22 **Listen again and complete these extracts from the interview.**

1 In 2005, the Bowens .... an idea for a 'green plug' that could .... electrical appliances automatically, for example when you leave your iron accidentally ....
....

2 I................... .... one of those. I think I'd save a lot of energy and money.

3 Besides, they were also .... for government loans designed for green start-ups.

4 Sorry to .... you, but how did they manage to raise the capital they needed, then?

5 Our listeners often .... us for help and advice on how to .... climate change by reducing energy consumption.

F **Match the phrases and multi-word verbs from Exercise E to these synonyms and explanations. Give the bare infinitive form of the verbs.**

1 interrupt ....

2 need ....

3 stop using a piece of equipment by adjusting the controls ....

4 go to someone for help ....

5 think of something ....

6 take the necessary action, e.g. in order to solve a problem ....

7 refuse ....

8 make a light or machine start working ....

Consultants

A   **Complete each sentence with the best word.**

1   Organisations often hire management consultants when they want to improve their
     .... *c* ....

    a)   scope   **b)**   objective   **c)**   performance

2   The client has to set a .... ; they have specified how long the consultant
     has to complete the assignment.

    a)   timescale   **b)**   timepiece   **c)**   timeshare

3   We have no doubts about our consultants' .... in the telecom field
     because they have worked on similar projects in various parts of the world.

    a)   knowledge   **b)**   expertise   **c)**   specialty

4   Consultants work with multiple clients so they are generally aware of industry best
     ....

    a)   performances   **b)**   practice   **c)**   skills

5   Data analysis technologies are playing an increasingly important role in improving
     the .... efficiency of health care systems.

    a)   operational   **b)**   practical   **c)**   professional

6   Our consultants estimate 18 months from the research stage to .... of
     the new network.

    a)   duplication   **b)**   concession   **c)**   implementation

7   When consultants and their clients talk of .... , they are referring to the
     key stages which must be completed on time and on budget for the project to meet
     expectations.

    a)   milestones   **b)**   achievements   **c)**   deliverables

8   The .... usually includes a description of the problem which has led the
     organisation to hire a consultant and sets out what has to be achieved.

    a)   agenda   **b)**   scope   **c)**   brief

9   Waverley Consulting provided .... and practical approaches that have
     resulted in a workplace culture that better aligns with our strategy.

    a)   audible   **b)**   tangible   **c)**   renewable

10   In the past, a consultancy's main .... on a project was generally the
     report.

    a)   competence   **b)**   deliverable   **c)**   assessment

11   If we'd had enough time and resources, I'm sure we could have done the work
     ....

    a)   start-up   **b)**   off-line   **c)**   in-house

12   Their consultants may charge exorbitant .... but their professionalism is
     unsurpassed.

    a)   fees   **b)**   wages   **c)**   costs

B **Match a word from box A with a word from box B to make suitable multi-word verbs to complete the sentences below.**

A	B
pile	out
plan	up
pack	out
go	up
circle	out
wrap	through
hammer	back
leave	up

1 E-mails have a tendency to ...pile up......... if you don't clean out your inbox regularly.

2 Back at my hotel after a day full of meetings and presentations, I .... my night, which will include the swimming pool, a quick dinner and preparing for tomorrow.

3 Let's .... at six, shall we? I want to go home early today.

4 The data I received is a real mess. I need to .... it carefully and clean it up.

5 'I don't think we can agree on all the points today, so let's leave it at that and I'll .... with you on the remaining issues in a couple of days.'

6 'It's getting late so I'd like to .... this meeting by mentioning that our client still has some questions regarding the proposed timescale.'

7 The two companies will take several months to .... an agreement for splitting the profits.

8 Always double-check your PowerPoint slides. You don't want to .... any important details or footnotes.

C **Complete this text with words formed from the words given.**

govern The board of directors of AIG has its own lawyer. The Morgan Stanley board has its own lawyer. In the tough new world of American corporate ....governance....[1], does every board need its own independent counsel?

liable In the post-Enron world, corporate directors face a raft of new duties – and new ....[2]. Some are turning to outside counsel – lawyers who work just for them and not for the management – to help them navigate the governance minefield. Does this mean independent legal advisers will become a fixture of American boardrooms? Or will most stick with the company's own lawyers to guide them through the battle zone?

depend For the past 30 years, independent directors have sought outside counsel to deal with situations where shareholders want to sue a company or in the case of a management buy-out or an ....[3] investigation after a scandal.

require / complex But recent changes to the rules of the Securities and Exchange Commission and stock exchange listing ....[4] vastly increase the legal ....[5] of the role of independent director. Legally challenged directors will need more advice to do their jobs – and they are bound to look for it from someone other than the general counsel.

power
agree
except But E. Norman Veasey – a ....[6] voice in corporate governance – ....[7]. He thinks special counsel for independent directors – or even for independent bodies such as the audit committee – should be 'the ....[8] not the rule'.

conscience
proliferate 'Most governance issues are matters of a ....[9] application of common sense,' he says. 'One does not need a ....[10] of counsel to do the right thing.'

A **Rewrite Speaker B's responses so that they use ellipsis and sound natural.**

1 A: Mr Raimes might arrive early.

B: I don't think he will arrive early, though.

I don't think he will, though.

2 A: Have you talked to Sue about the contract?

B: Yes, I have talked to Sue about the contract.

....

3 A: What time does the meeting start?

B: The meeting starts at nine thirty.

....

4 A: Like to go out tonight after Werner's presentation?

B: Yes, I'd love to go out tonight after Werner's presentation. Do you have anywhere in mind?

....

5 A: Should anyone else have been sent a copy of the report?

B: Well, Svetlana should have been sent a copy of the report.

....

6 A: Will you check the PowerPoint slides?

B: I have checked the PowerPoint slides already.

....

7 A: Is Jane going to the conference?

B: I have no idea whether Jane is going to the conference.

....

8 A: Will you be able to attend?

B: I hope I will be able to attend.

....

B **Rewrite the following as conditional sentences.**

1 We were not given sufficient time and resources. That's why we couldn't do the research in-house.

If we *had been given sufficient time and resources, we could have done the research in-house.*

2 I know they don't have the necessary skills to do the work in-house. That's why they have to rely on an outside expert.

If they ....

....

3 I was not well prepared. So now I don't feel good about the negotiation.

If I ....

....

4 He isn't a good communicator. We can't ask him to conduct the negotiation.

If he ....

....

5 They didn't set a realistic timescale. The project wasn't completed on time.

If they ....

....

6 Pity I wasn't able to negotiate better terms.

   I wish I ....

   ....

7 We didn't bring in a consultant. The crisis wasn't defused very quickly.

   If we ....

   ....

8 He is an inefficient manager. His projects are not on budget.

   If he ....

   ....

9 I didn't realise my client was dissatisfied. I didn't make a substantial concession.

   If I ....

   ....

10 We weren't clear about what we wanted. Now we aren't pleased with what we've got.

   If we ....

   ....

C **Complete the second sentence in each pair so that it has approximately the same meaning as the first sentence. Use exactly *three* words, including the word given.**

1 Providing that you deliver this month, we agree to cover insurance and
   freight.   (**condition**)

   We agree to cover insurance and freight ..... *on condition that* .... you deliver
   this month.

2 If you are interested in our training solutions, please contact our local
   office.   (**should**)

   .... interested in our training solutions, please
   contact our local office.

3 If we don't get some results soon, we won't see this project through.   (**unless**)

   We won't see this project through .... some results
   soon.

4 We'll launch a new project if you're on time and on budget on this occasion.   (**long**)

   .... you're on time and on budget on this occasion,
   we'll launch a new project.

5 You may need further information, so I'm going to give you my contact details.   (**case**)

   I'll give you my contact details .... need further
   information.

A **Complete the e-mail with words and phrases from the box.**

and then	~~as per~~	but of course	however
I'm afraid this	in addition	let's	looking forward

> **To:** Rolix.HR@dunanet.hu
> **Subject:** Screening candidates
>
> Hello Nora,
>
> *As per*.........¹ your instructions, we have screened all 18 consultants who expressed interest in retraining our Accounts personnel and submitted a project proposal ....² shortlisted three.
>
> ....³ meet as soon as you can make it to discuss their profiles and assess the suitability of their proposals together.
>
> ....⁴ won't be particularly straightforward as all three show a thorough understanding of our needs and a clear picture of what the outcome of the consultancy would be.
>
> ....⁵, their referees are unanimous in praising their ability to diagnose problems, present workable solutions, and implement those solutions effectively.
>
> ....⁶, they do differ noticeably with regard to the fees they charge.
>
> ....⁷, I don't want to influence your decision too much at this stage!
>
> ....⁸ to your reply.
>
> Yours,
>
> Bert

B ◀)) 23 **Listen to five different people talking about a mistake they made when hiring a consultant. Decide which mistake each speaker made.**

- Write one letter, (**a–h**), next to the number of the speaker.
- Do not use any letter more than once.

Speaker 1 ....

Speaker 2 ....

Speaker 3 ....

Speaker 4 ....

Speaker 5 ....

a) failure to enquire about the consultant's other commitments

b) failure to ask the consultant to sign a letter of confidentiality

c) failure to establish who pays for certain expenses

d) failure to find out whether the work can be done in-house

e) failure to establish clear goal and objectives

f) failure to introduce the consultants to the staff

g) failure to plan for knowledge transfer

h) failure to specify concrete project deliverables

C ◀))23 **Listen again and decide what the main consequence of each mistake was.**

- Write one letter, (a–h), next to the number of the speaker.
- Do not use any letter more than once.

Speaker 1 ....   a)   a feeling of helplessness and dependence

Speaker 2 ....   b)   the consultant was dismissed

Speaker 3 ....   c)   a manager resigned

Speaker 4.....................   d)   an overspent budget

Speaker 5 ....   e)   being overtaken by a rival

     f)   the deadline was not met

     g)   the staff perceived the consultants as a menace

     h)   a dispute over payment

D **Rearrange the words to make expressions used in negotiations.**

1 I'll / can / see / what / I / do.
I'll..... *see what I can* .....do.

2 I / look / could / I / suppose / into / it.
I... into it.

3 I / should / be / that / think / doable.
I... doable.

4 I'll / from / wait / to / you / hear / then.
I'll... then.

5 I'd / check / my / supervisor / have / with / to / first.
I'd... first.

6 She'd / terms / confirm / the / payment / to / have / , / you / see.
She'd... , you see.

7 I / could / if / a / wondering / you / was / deliver / bit / sooner.
I... bit sooner.

8 Maybe / could / at / talk / little / we / terms / a / payment / about / this / point?
Maybe... this point?

◀))24 **Listen and check your answers. Then listen again and practise saying the sentences.**

E ◀))25 **Listen and complete these conditional sentences.**

1 .... agree to their terms if..................... .... you.

2 If..................... .... better prepared,..................... ....
felt more confident.

3 The project..................... .... successful if..................... set a more
realistic timescale.

4 I don't think..................... .... able to solve our problems unless
.... hire an independent consultant.

5 If..................... .... a better communicator, I'm sure.....................
.... asked to conduct the negotiation.

6 If..................... genuinely concerned about those difficulties,..................... bring
in a consultant.

◀))25 **Now listen again and practise the sentences, paying special attention to the contracted forms.**

Strategy

A **Complete each set of sentences with the same word.**

1 Successful companies are able to ..*draw*......... on the talents of the best people they can find – whether they employ them or not.

I still need to to ..*draw*......... up a brief agenda for tomorrow's meeting.

Can I to ..*draw*......... your attention to the second graph?

2 This year's .... of growth is expected to be twice that of last year.

According to many surveys, the job satisfaction .... is as high as 76 per cent.

Observers say Indian companies are ready to accept a lower .... of return than western companies in order to secure a strategic asset.

3 Their salaries .... from €65,000 to €90,000.

The majority of their customers are in the 17–25 age ....

For over 50 years, Ross & Franks has served a wide .... of customer needs from food to furniture, clothes to car insurance.

4 TCB Engineering's annual .... showed a loss last year of €2 million.

It's important that our marketing strategy focuses on multiple key areas, including food, which .... for 30 per cent of our turnover.

We haven't researched it ourselves, but Central Asia is a promising market by all ....

5 Mayer is fighting to weaken Renco's .... on 45 per cent of the specialty chemicals market.

Owing to insufficient funding, the project had to be put on ....

We're going to .... a meeting to brainstorm a new marketing strategy for R&F.

6 It seems that, quite often, the oil price has only a temporary effect on consumer ....

In the booming 1990s Marconi went on a .... spree to buy up various telco equipment companies.

The survey shows that many highly qualified women have non-linear careers, ... part of them in jobs with reduced hours or responsibility.

7 Consultants predict that most companies' growth levels are unlikely to .... 10 per cent.

India has managed to .... a $40bn agreement to import LNG from Iran.

With that new order, we now think this year's sales budget is within our ....

8 As their strategy was going nowhere, they decided to .... tack.

I only had about three euros in small ....

Well-run businesses are alive to social .... and shifting customer preferences.

9 As our bank is a provider of .... funding, the return for us is merely the interest that we are paid on the loan.

Dave was so heavily in .... that he had to sell off his house and car.

Although national .... levels have dropped, Brazil still depends on foreign savings to finance itself.

B Match a word from box A with a word from box B to complete the sentences below.

A	B
company	care
economic	advantage
mission	culture
staff	turnover
strategic	statement
competitive	planning
customer	outlook

1 The Chief Executive of Google is adamant that the ...*company* ...*culture*..., which allows engineers freedom to create new products and services, will not change.

2 High-trust organisations benefit from better communications, higher efficiency, greater employee commitment and lower ....

3 Companies do need a strategy for growth, even in periods of recession, in order to ensure a healthy recovery and gain a .... over their rivals.

4 Long-term .... is essential for any company: it plots where the company wants to go and how it's going to get there.

5 We need a new strategy because the world has changed, markets are unpredictable and the .... is uncertain.

6 To manage the expected increase in support calls after it launched the Xperia X1 smartphone, Sony Ericsson created a dedicated .... phone number specifically for those users.

7 A .... is meant to communicate an organisation's aims to customers, employees and shareholders.

C Complete the extract from a chairman's letter to shareholders with verbs from the box.

increased	added	implemented	issued
~~marked~~	named	remained	strengthened

This past year has been ...*marked*...[1] by many achievements that, as a result of the hard work and dedication of our employees, led us to become a truly multi-dimensional company with expanded products and services that provide new opportunities for continued growth.

Here are some details of our achievements:

Strategic acquisitions

We completed two strategic acquisitions that have significantly ....[2] to our revenue opportunities.

We broadened our product offering.

Financial and operating performance

We ....[3] both operating profit and net income.

We ....[4] our balance sheet.

We ....[5] profitable while absorbing acquisition and integration costs.

Corporate communication and visibility

We ....[6] a large number of press releases to provide key news on our progress.

We ....[7] a more proactive investor communications strategy.

We were ....[8] by Aubert & Stein as one of the 10 fastest growing technology companies in the region.

A **For each sentence, indicate in which of the underlined items there is a mistake, then write the correction in the table below. The first one has been done for you.**

1 Business intelligence <u>has been part of</u>[(a)] the enterprise software landscape for as long as 30 years but, <u>unlike other</u>[(b)] key business software markets, <u>they have</u>[(c)] been slow to mature.

2 The strategic planning <u>is being</u>[(a)] led by two vice-chairmen, Tom Muller and Dan Roberts, <u>each of who</u>[(b)] is regarded as a prime candidate <u>to lead</u>[(c)] the company, <u>along with</u>[(d)] chief counsel Anne Costello.

3 The company's plans <u>to cut</u>[(a)] its sales force have already been presented <u>to its board</u>[(b)] of directors and are <u>been fine-tuned</u>[(c)] in readiness for next week's announcement.

4 Financial analysts <u>called for</u>[(a)] heavy cost-cutting in administration and a moderate reduction of the sales force, <u>argued that</u>[(b)] such measures could save <u>the company up</u>[(c)] to $2bn over the next five years.

5 <u>While</u>[(a)] senior executives talk about retooling the company, i.e., changing sales practices and <u>using</u>[(b)] technology to become <u>closer to</u>[(c)] the customer, a less radical package of measures <u>are expected</u>[(d)] on Tuesday.

6 <u>Although most</u>[(a)] of the enterprise software and infrastructure vendors do not break down revenues by individual product lines, the importance of business intelligence <u>on the enterprise</u>[(b)] software companies cannot <u>be overstated</u>[(c)].

Sentence	Incorrect item	Correction
1	........(c)........	......it has......
2	....	....
3	....	....
4	....	....
5	....	....
6	....	....

B **Complete the second sentence in each pair so that it has approximately the same meaning as the first sentence. Use between *three* and *five* words, including the word given.**

1 Providing that no one is too critical, people generally feel comfortable about being creative.   (**condition**)

People generally feel comfortable about being creative *on condition that* no one is too critical.

2 It is better not to raise the issue of advertising costs at the meeting.   (**brought**)

The issue of advertising costs should .... at the meeting.

3 That our new strategy is going nowhere is something that must be recognised and dealt with.   (**face**)

We must .... that our new strategy is going nowhere.

4 It lies with the manager to evaluate the project proposals.   (**responsibility**)

Evaluating the project proposals ....

5 The number of men promoted to head of department was double that of women.   (**twice**)

There were .... promoted to head of department as women.

6 Our competitor's strategy is a lot more effective than ours.   (**nearly**)

Our strategy .... as our competitor's.

7 There were no problems whatsoever during the initial phase of the negotiations.   (**plan**)

Everything .... during the initial phase of the negotiations.

8 The strategy will not succeed unless it is carefully planned.   (**essential**)

Careful .... the success of the strategy.

9 I regret not taking their advice.   (**only**)

If .... their advice.

10 Our currency should be revalued at last.   (**time**)

It is .... revalued.

C **Read the passage below about the need for a new type of marketing strategy in Japan.**

- In most of the lines **1–13** there is **one extra word** which does not fit. Some lines, however, are correct.
- If a line is **correct**, put a tick in the space provided.
- If there is an **extra word** in the line, write that word in the space provided.

Yayoi, a 24-year-old who works in an office at a Japanese company, is obsessed with   1 ....✓.......

stars. In a homemade video, she shows off her star candles, a star brooch and even of an   2 ....of.......

ear cleaner adorned with a star charm. For her, when it comes up to stars, money is no   3 ....

object. In Japan, there is a name for such a product to fanatic: *otaku*. Increasingly, these   4 ....

individuals are regarded as a normal – if not necessary – component of Japan's cultural   5 ....

fabric. Advertisers and marketers are waking up early to the innumerable young people   6 ....

who belong to subcultures and have a great deal of the money to spend on items they   7 ....

feel help define their lifestyle. Japan has become a very hotbed for youth trends that   8 ....

influence a young people throughout the world. In addition, there have been important   9 ....

structural shifts in the youth market. The breakdown of the lifetime and employment   10 ....

system has given rise to a category of young adults dubbed *freeters* in the media.   11 ....

Freeters may or may not have attended to college but they do hold down a number of   12 ....

part-time jobs while pursuing their dreams – whether as a guitarist in a punk band or if   13 ....

studying to be a beautician.

A Complete the mission statements with items from the box.

> of advancing and applying
> helping individuals, businesses and communities
> considers the environment
> strives to be the global leader
> to offer
> make the most of

1 adidas Group .... in the sporting goods industry with sports brands built on a passion for sports and a sporting lifestyle. (adidas Group)

2 To experience the joy .... technology for the benefit of the public. (Sony)

3 Ikea's mission is .... a wide range of home furnishing items of good design and function, excellent quality and durability, at prices so low that the majority of people can afford to buy them. (Ikea)

4 Nokia will empower everyone to share and .... their life by offering irresistible personal experiences. (Nokia)

5 Our vision is to be the world's mobile communications leader – enriching customers' lives, ... be more connected in a mobile world. (Vodafone)

6 Delivering energy in a way that provides social benefits and .... (Shell Oman)

B Complete each sentence with the best linker.

1 They were fiercely debating the issue of growth. ....*a*........., their discussion never got out of hand.

a) However   b) Despite   c) Besides

2 KPC Systems remains a substantial force. ...., there are signs that its market value is shrinking.

a) Even though   b) In addition   c) On the other hand

3 .... a difficult operating environment in some of our key businesses, our performance improved significantly.

a) Nevertheless   b) Despite   c) However

4 Their sales of cosmetics began to decline as fewer women purchased products sold door-to-door. ...., their cosmetics had little appeal with teenagers.

a) However   b) In addition   c) On the other hand

5 .... the Middle East, the West has now discovered another obsession: the rising power of China.

a) Furthermore   b) Although   c) Besides

6 .... we are very positive about the potential of the Angolan operations, we remain extremely cautious in our approach.

a) Even though   b) However   c) In addition

7 It has been a difficult year. ...., earnings per share increased by 15 per cent.

a) Nevertheless   b) Besides   c) Although

8 Our efficiency has earned us a place among the top ten software companies in this country. ...., investors appear to have full confidence in our capacity to grow our business.

a) Yet   b) However   c) Furthermore

C ◀)) 26 **Listen to how certain sounds are linked together in these phrases.**

1 my‿office
2 try‿again
3 they‿arrived

4 we‿agreed
5 pay‿off
6 free‿enterprise

Explanation

If a word ends in /iː/, /aɪ/ or /eɪ/ and the next word begins with a vowel sound, we often add /j/ to link them when we speak quickly. For example, *my office* becomes /maɪjɒfɪs/, *they arrived* becomes /ðeɪjəraɪvd/, etc.

D ◀)) 27 **Indicate where similar links could be made in these sentences. Then listen to check your answers.**

1 They agreed to come to my office.
2 Would May or June be all right?
3 Let's try again in a day or two.

◀)) 27 **Listen again and practise each sentence after you hear it.**

E ◀)) 28 **Listen to how Speaker B highlights the word which is most significant in the context.**

1 A: The team members aren't particularly cooperative.

   B: But they are <u>creative</u>.

2 A: The team members aren't particularly creative.

   B: But they <u>are</u> creative.

F **Underline the words Speaker B will highlight in these conversations.**

1 A: Thanks for that book on strategic planning. Great stuff!

   B: I thought you'd like it.

2 A: That book isn't worth the paper it's printed on.

   B: I thought you'd like it.

3 A: The management can't be held responsible for this failure.

   B: Well, I believe the management is responsible.

4 A: Who would you say is to blame for this failure?

   B: Well, I believe the management is responsible.

5 A: Do they show any cynicism about the idea?

   B: Yeah. I find them very cynical.

6 A: So you're disappointed with our new team members?

   B: Yeah. I find them very cynical.

7 A: Does the new product appeal to teenagers?

   B: I'm afraid it has no appeal to teenagers.

8 A: Which segment doesn't find our new product appealing, then?

   B: I'm afraid it has no appeal to teenagers.

◀)) 29 **Listen to check your answers. Then listen again and take Speaker B's role.**

WORD POWER

A **Complete this crossword puzzle.**

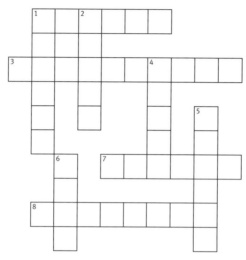

Across

1   Companies are taking advantage of viral marketing including blogging and
    .... networking in place of more conventional marketing. (6)

3   .... is the skill of finding and following a path through Internet
    websites. (10)

7   Many will remember 2000 as the year of the .... crash. (6)

8   .... refers to the sets of programs that tell a computer how to do a particular
    job. (8)

Down

1   There are signs that in the next few years, the Google .... monopoly may
    become even more apparent in more countries. (6)

2   These days, with a single ...., you can order practically anything
    online. (5)

4   A..................... is an entry posted on the microblogging service Twitter. (5)

5   Internet users can now easily swap music files .... on their
    computers. (6)

6   A....................., or weblog, is a webpage containing information or opinions from
    a particular person or about a particular subject, to which new information is added
    regularly. (4)

B **Complete each sentence with the best word.**

1 Social networking websites are often used by companies to communicate with their customers, to solve problems or to ....*a*......... a brewing crisis.

   a) defuse   **b)** turn on   **c)** erupt

2 Some companies have used social media such as Twitter to .... out public relations fires before they spread.

   a) take   **b)** throw   **c)** put

3 The company's social media team attempts to track down dissatisfied customers and then contacts them in order to .... amends for poor service or faulty products.

   a) give   **b)** make   **c)** hold

4 By .... discount alerts on Twitter, Dell has generated more than $1m in sales.

   a) emitting   **b)** activating   **c)** broadcasting

5 The company's blog resolution team .... the Web for comments, both positive and negative, on our products and services.

   a) trawl   **b)** click   **c)** tweet

6 All our staff have an intimate familiarity with social media, which enables them to be .... to the needs and wants of our customers.

   a) arranged   **b)** attuned   **c)** showed up

7 The extraordinary expansion of social media has brought about a radical .... in the way companies communicate with their customers.

   a) solution   **b)** shift   **c)** crash

8 A growing number of companies are putting together teams of high-level employees whose role is to .... with social media.

   a) familiarise   **b)** involve   **c)** engage

9 Other savings can be .... through the Web's ability to reach many people at once.

   a) realised   **b)** resolved   **c)** done

10 eBay, an online .... site which was founded in 1995, enables Internet users to trade with each other.

   a) booking   **b)** search   **c)** auction

C **Match these sentence halves.**

1 Despite their very competitive prices,   **a)** has kept ticket prices relatively low.

2 The company's involvement in controversial arms deals   **b)** starting a dotcom is no guarantee you will make money hand over fist.

3 As our supplier was unable to meet the deadline for delivery,   **c)** they failed to retain their customer base.

4 There may be lots of success stories, but   **d)** they have always lived up to our expectations.

5 So far, cut-throat competition   **e)** we had to cancel our order.

6 Their after-sales service may not have an excellent reputation, but   **f)** severely damaged its reputation.

A **For each sentence, indicate in which of the underlined items there is a mistake, then write the correction in the table below.**

1 Although a lot of customers <u>still lacking confidence</u>[a] in Internet security, there is <u>no denying that</u> [b] online shopping is growing in popularity in <u>many Western countries</u>[c].

2 Not only <u>does e-business enable</u>[a] companies to <u>present their goods</u>[b] in a more attractive fashion and to handle orders online but <u>they also result</u>[c] in improved margins for them.

3 The authorities <u>have its reasons</u>[a] for stopping online gambling advertisements and blocking people <u>from using</u>[b] credit cards <u>to bet online</u>[c].

4 The use of e-mail has spread <u>so rapidly</u>[a] <u>since the last 15 years</u>[b] that it is <u>hard to imagine</u>[c] life without it.

Sentence	Incorrect item	Correction
1	....	....
2	....	....
3	....	....
4	....	....

B **Here is the first part of a *Financial Times* article by Lucy Kellaway. Complete it with suitable words.**

Business metaphors

The gloves are off. The creators of business metaphors have been pulling their punches for more than a decade but have now come out swinging. There is a new metaphor in the management ring and, just in case you are too punch-drunk after so many idioms to have guessed what it is, here's the knockout blow: it's boxing.

The latest Harvard Business Review contains an 11-page article telling us that ...*the*...[1] best way to survive financial meltdown and global recession is to be like Muhammad Ali when he met George Foreman for their Rumble in the Jungle in Kinshasa, Zaire.

What the renowned boxer's performance teaches us about thriving in turbulent markets ....[2] that we must all be agile and we have to absorb blows. The point is helpfully summarised by various charts, diagrams and a two-by-two matrix with agility up one side ....[3] absorption along the other.

Curiously, the HBR doesn't mention any ....[4] the things about boxing that immediately come to my mind when I think of it. In boxing, you get beaten to a pulp – which must ring a bell with anyone ....[5] is now working on the economic front line. In boxing, you are quite likely to wind up with brain damage ....[6] you go on doing it for long enough – and, if things get much worse in the economy, this too may come to ring a bell.

Recently, I read that this bloody sport has become newly fashionable as an activity doled out by the authorities to young delinquents to distract them ....[7] drug-taking and knife crime. However, ...[8] discover that boxing is now the very latest fashion for management theorists is more surprising still.

The HBR article brings to ....[9] end 15 years of peace, love and political correctness by the purveyors of management metaphor. It is the first evidence I have seen from the management guff industry ....[10] 'soft' is finally on its way out and 'hard' is on its way in.

FT Publishing
FINANCIAL TIMES

C Complete the second part of Lucy Kellaway's article below with some of the sentences a–g. You will only need five of the seven sentences.

a) There have been ape theories, geese theories and even frog theories.

b) We need to gain a fresh insight into the use of metaphors in business.

c) The idea of a business as a stream of DNA always struck me as moronic.

d) Even more popular than music as a metaphor has been sport.

e) We need to take fewer risks.

f) The great leader must not tell his players how to play but let them jam, be creative and let it all hang out.

g) As we all know, the main role of DNA molecules is the long-term storage of information.

Since I started following these things in the early 1990s, there have been three different sorts of metaphors wheeled out by gurus to help explain and prescribe business behaviour, all benign. The first were musical metaphors. There was the idea of a company as an orchestra, with the chief executive as the conductor. Each knowledge worker scraped away at her fiddle or blew his horn and the maestro waved a thin stick to bring them together in perfect time and harmony.

This metaphor was popular for a while but, as the Internet grew, gurus got groovier and decided that classical was out and jazz was in. ....[1] Presently, even this seemed too square and in 2002 a Swedish writer said that the CEO should be like a DJ, mixing records to match the mood on the dance floor.

...................[2] Most of these have been based on the idea that business is a team effort (which we know it isn't, really). Football, rugby, rowing, cricket and baseball have all taken their turn as trendy management theories.

Sports without teams also get a look-in in the metaphor market, in particular golf and a weird sled race with huskies that came into vogue a few years ago.

The third, and daftest, seam of management metaphor comes from science ....[3]

The point about a person's DNA is that it does not change. The point about companies and business conditions is that they do. It may be more plausible for gurus to talk the language of evolution and describe companies as complex adaptive systems – or it might be helpful if I could understand what they were driving at. A metaphor is meant to simplify, not to obfuscate.

Finally, there have been some outliers that fit none of the three categories: management as akin to being a top chef in a big kitchen and management likened to animal behaviour. ....[4] The softest – and most famous – was the wretched mouse with the wretched cheese in the parable, *Who Moved My Cheese?*

All of these metaphors have one thing in common: they are perfectly useless. I defy anyone to show how any of them has helped us understand how businesses behave or help us get better at running them.

Metaphors can be helpful in grasping something when the thing is terribly complicated. So, when Einstein was explaining relativity, he used a train and a clock to help us understand something that would otherwise have been beyond most of us.

By comparison, business – or the theory of business – is terribly simple. We know what we need to survive in troubled times and it does not take 11 pages of boxing parallels to tell us. We need to cut costs. ....[5] We need to conserve cash. We need to pull out of markets in which we are not successful. We need to fly economy – or not at all. There are two things that we don't need to do: float like a butterfly or sting like a bee.

FT Publishing
FINANCIAL TIMES

A **Write a report (maximum 150 words) on the chart below.**

- The bar chart below shows the approximate percentage of households with Internet access in four different countries in 2007 and in 2009.

- Use the information from the chart to summarise the changes.

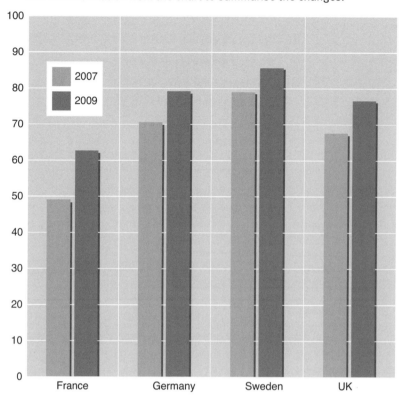

B **Match these sentence halves.**

Protect your business against spam

1	Unsolicited commercial communications, or 'spam',	a)	for their personal and professional communications.
2	Over the last ten years, spam has grown	b)	for service providers, businesses and end-users alike.
3	The cost of spam to the global economy is estimated	c)	will therefore welcome the OECD's 'Anti-Spam Toolkit'.
4	This is now causing enormous financial costs and losses in productivity	d)	has turned into one of the major problems affecting today's digital environment.
5	Users are increasingly dependent on the Internet and e-mail	e)	thereby hindering the development of the information society.
6	Unfortunately, spam is sapping user confidence and trust in online activities,	f)	to account for almost 80 per cent of total e-mail traffic, with spammers sending hundreds of millions of messages per day.
7	All stakeholders in the digital economy	g)	at over 20 billion euros per year.
8	The toolkit is an initiative designed	h)	can be found at http://www.oecd-antispam.org.
9	More information about the OECD's work on spam	i)	to develop cross-border anti-spam strategies.

C ◀») **30 Listen to the commentaries. For each bar chart 1–6, decide which statement a), b) or c) is correct.**

1 ....

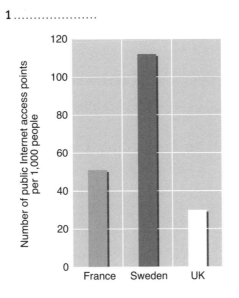

2 ....

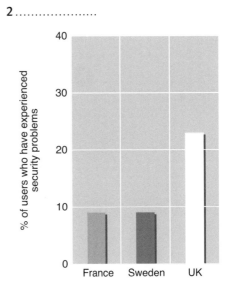

3 ....

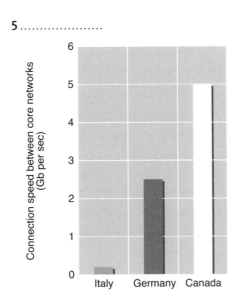

4 ....

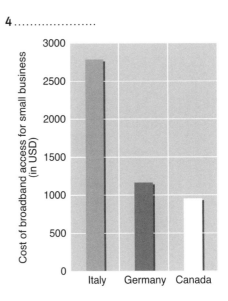

5 ....

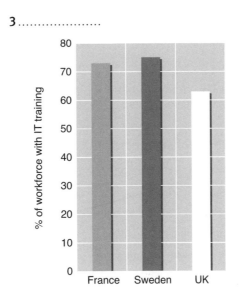

6 ....

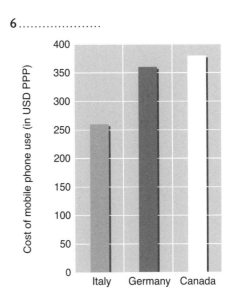

New business

A **Complete the word or phrase in the sentences.**

1 _ _t_ _pr_ _ _ _ _s_ _ _ could be described as the drive people need to take risks and start a company.

2 Money used to start a new company, project or activity is often called _ _ _d c_ _ _t_ _.

3 A sales _ _t_ _ is what sales people say about a product to persuade people to buy it.

4 A business _r_ _ _ is a sum of money given by a government to get new businesses off the ground.

5 The movement of money into and out of a company is called the _ _s_ _l_ _.

6 P_ _s_ _ _r_ _c_ is the ability to continue despite setbacks, financial insecurity and risk and is one of the main qualities of an entrepreneur.

7 A recent study suggests that one in six Britons aged 46–65 hopes to embark on a new b_ _ _ _ _ss v_ _t_ _ _ rather than retire.

8 When starting a new business, you need to think about how you are going to _ _ff_ _ _ _ _ _ _ _ yourself from the competition.

9 A p_ _t_t_ _ _ is the first form that a newly designed product has.

10 Since we started, we've definitely improved our production processes and managed to reduce costs, production and _ _l_v_r_ times.

B **Complete each set of sentences with the same word.**

1 The company's chief executive has been on medical leave since May, when she suffered a ..... *stroke* ......

   Finding a business angel in less than a week was quite a ...... *stroke* ..... of luck.

   We had two problems, but we managed to solve both of them at a ...... *stroke* .....

2 We had been advised to attend a trade .... called The Nursery Fair but we made a mistake and booked one called Nursery World instead.

   It is essential that we try to .... an interest in our customers' needs.

   Could you .... me the right way to do this?

3 The .... of exports was up 4 per cent on the previous three months.

   According to the Chamber of Shipping, 95 per cent of UK trade by .... and 90 per cent by value is carried by sea.

   AB Inbev is the world's largest brewer by ....

4 Environmental campaigners have stepped up their fight against coal-fired power with an attempt to block a .... carrying fuel to the Kingsnorth power station in Kent.

   The aorta is the blood .... which leaves the heart with high pressure oxygenated blood, which is then sent round the body.

   Mandy Haberman came up with a clever design for a non-spill child's drinking ...., called the Anywayup Cup.

5 All we are asking for is a .... wage.

   I won't carry on working such long hours because it's not .... on my family.

   Representatives from book publishing and multimedia companies from all over the world come to the Frankfurt Book .... in order to negotiate international publishing rights and licensing fees.

6 The company was forced to .... one range of cereals after several packets were found to be contaminated.

Total .... is the ability of a person to remember the past accurately in seemingly complete detail.

'It was a very successful event, hundreds of people wanted to talk to us,' Mandy and Jeff ....

7 When you leave the hotel, please leave your key at the .... desk.

We are holding a special .... for the Japanese trade delegation.

Mandy says that the positive .... to her product was unexpected.

8 Please inform us if there are any .... changes in your plans.

There is a .... difference between the number of Internet users now and ten years ago.

It is .... that the time when we cut welfare is almost always during recessions.

9 On .... reflection we have decided to decline their offer.

A .... market is one where growth is relatively low and there are fewer competitors than before.

This exciting position would suit a .... personal assistant with computer skills.

10 Becoming self-employed can be a bit of a gamble, as it certainly does not always .... off.

Welco has been trying to raise cash to .... its debts.

Clients who do not .... on time can cause serious problems with your cash flow.

C **Complete the text with the best words.**

One of the keys to a successful start-up is personal and professional networking. New entrepreneurs sometimes tend to be too concerned about how much money they will be able to ......b......[1], when in fact who invests is often more important than how much is invested. They should be asking themselves whether the investing company has the right connections with large companies, sources of money and ....[2] of distribution.

Secondly, it is important to realise that very few people have all the skills, experience, contacts or reputation that are required to get a business ....[3] and running. This means that in order to make your ....[4], you need to find a business partner whose talents complement yours.

The next key skill is the ability to let ....[5] and to delegate. This involves being able to gauge other people's ....[6] and creating opportunities for them to move up and run organisations on their own.

1	a)	rouse	b)	raise	c)	arise	d)	rise
2	a)	channels	b)	roads	c)	avenues	d)	canals
3	a)	alive	b)	high	c)	strong	d)	up
4	a)	success	b)	goal	c)	aim	d)	mark
5	a)	down	b)	do	c)	go	d)	off
6	a)	risk	b)	potential	c)	venture	d)	skill

A **Complete the text below with the noun phrases a–h.**

a) a list of potential buyers

b) a long-term aim and purpose

c) an expectation of return on that capital

d) different levels of maturity

e) an initial public offering*

f) the identity of the company

g) the Italian coffee café experience

h) the sale of the entire business

*an occasion when a company issues shares on a stock market for the first time

---

All businesses must have ......b......¹. It may be to change the way people listen to music or to deliver ....² to the rest of the world. That purpose creates the focus and ....³. It is this identity that ultimately defines the company itself as a product that may one day be purchased.

Some people start businesses with no intention of ever selling. If this is your plan, you must ask yourself if the business will require outside capital. You cannot attract capital without ....⁴: if the capital is an equity investment, it is likely the investor will eventually want to exit from the investment, which often means....................⁵.

Returns can, of course, be delivered without selling a business. Entrepreneurs can borrow money rather than sell an equity stake. But they have to be in a position to borrow and many start-up entrepreneurs are not.

With equity investors, the choice is usually between a trade sale and flotation. I am a great believer in building companies that retain the option to do either: the value achieved in a trade sale is enhanced if it has the choice of floating instead; while preparing for

....................⁶ frequently triggers a buyer's interest.

Planning for an IPO is influenced by external forces: sectors blow hot and cold and markets demand ....⁷ at different times. But, generally, it is necessary to develop the company to a level where it can forecast the steady growth in turnover and profits that is rewarded by the market. Planning for a trade sale requires different tactics. Companies are advised to draw up ....⁸, even as they are designing the business.

B **Use a cleft sentence each time to emphasise a different piece of information.**

In December 2009, Turkish Airlines placed an order with Airbus for 20 new planes.

1 (October) *Sorry, I'm afraid you're mistaken. It was in December 2009 that Turkish Airlines placed their order.*

2 (50) *It was 20 new planes that they placed an order for.*

3 (Emirates) ....

4 (2008) ....

5 (Boeing) ....

6 (airframes) ....

C **Complete the sentences with the nouns from the box.**

damage decision difference difficulty ~~increase~~ solution

1 We expected a bigger ...*increase*... in sales before summer.

2 The presenter was unable to explain the .... between a licence and a franchise.

3 The company could not reach a .... on whether or not to postpone its stock market flotation.

4 We hope to find a .... to the problem of high employee turnover.

5 Unethical investments can cause a lot of .... to a company's image.

6 A lot of new businesses have great .... in attracting capital.

D **Complete the noun phrases with a suitable preposition.**

1 Quite a few banks still have a negative attitude .... Internet transactions.

2 They were unable to think of an alternative .... selling an equity stake.

3 Deltellcom reported a 33 per cent rise .... first half profits before tax.

4 There has been a very strong demand .... loans to buy houses over the last six months.

5 We had no idea what they would say in their reply .... our offer.

6 The bank manager did not make a single comment .... my business plan.

E **Read the passage below about new business.**

- In most of the lines **1–16** there is **one extra word** which does not fit. Some lines, however, are correct.

- If a line is **correct,** put a tick in the space provided.

- If there is an **extra word** in the line, write that word in the space provided.

There are four key ingredients to high-growth start-ups: an innovation, a good team, the	1 ....✓............
right market opportunity and the right financing of strategy. Obviously, they all tie	2 ....of..........
together but it is possible to have a look at each one them separately.	3 ....
The first ingredient is innovation. Let's start with a misunderstanding. Innovation is not	4 ....
merely the invention. Yes, it can be a new widget, a new technology, a new drug or a	5 ....
new toy. But it can also be a new service or a new way of operating and an old business.	6 ....
Three great examples of operating an old business in a new way have become such	7 ....
global brands: Amazon, eBay and Dell Computers. None of them invented it; all of them	8 ....
innovated. Amazon offered a better way to buy books, eBay found a new way to sell	9 ....
used goods and Dell found a way to lower the cost of a personal computer down.	10 ....
What they had much in common from the start was their approach to their business.	11 ....
Each asked the key question: 'What is the problem about I am solving?'	12 ....
It may seem an obvious but that question cannot be answered in isolation. It means	13 ....
talking to prospective customers. They are the people who have the problem you want to	14 ....
solve them. They understand the problem and you have to understand it better than they	15 ....
do it. You must talk to more than one and you have to talk to them more than once.	16 ....

A   Put the sentences in this letter in the correct order.

Sigma
Office Solutions

21 Cranbrook Crescent

London EC2 5PE

17 May

Ms Elida Lonza

Purchasing Manager

Display Graphics International

Water Lane

Macclesfield, Cheshire

SK10 6YH

a)   Dear Ms Lonza,   `1`

b)   However, if you have already settled the invoice in the meantime, please disregard this reminder.

c)   In view of our good business relationship so far, we are disappointed in this delay as well as in not receiving an explanation of why you have not cleared the balance.

d)   Please find enclosed a copy of the invoice, together with a copy of our first reminder.

e)   We also have to bring to your attention the fact that our first reminder, which we sent on 7 May, has remained unanswered.

f)   We are writing concerning invoice No. P5K/200 for £1,250, which should have been settled a month ago.

g)   We look forward to your payment.

h)   We must now insist that you settle the account by 30 May at the latest.

Yours sincerely,

Ron Blackwell

Accountant

B   Write a reply to the letter in Exercise A.

In your reply, make sure you:

- apologise for the delay
- provide an explanation for the delay
- give details of what you have done or intend to do
- give Sigma Office Solutions reassurances that such delays will not happen again.

DISPLAY GRAPHICS INTERNATIONAL

Water Lane · Macclesfield · Cheshire · SK10 6YH

Sigma Office Solutions

FAO Mr Ron Blackwell

21 Cranbrook Crescent

London EC2 5PE

19 May

Dear Mr Blackwell,

With reference …

C 🔊 **31 Listen to how Speaker B uses stress to correct Speaker A.**

1 A: … So the reference number of the invoice is 47/AP.

   B: Sorry, no. 47/IP.

2 A: … and you are saying your original order was for forty units.

   B: No, no. It was fourteen units. One four.

D **Underline the part that Speaker B will stress to correct Speaker A in these telephone conversations.**

1 A: Let me just go over that. The supplier's name was Rod Jowett. J-O-W-E-double T.

   B: No. The surname's spelt J-O-W-I-double T.

2 A: … and you said you expected delivery by June the third, is that right?

   B: No. In fact, delivery was due on June the first. So it's already three days late.

3 A: I just need to enter your details on my computer. So, Edmond Keeler, E-D-M-O-N-D …

   B: Sorry. My first name is spelt E-D-M-U-N-D.

4 A: So you are saying that the invoice is three weeks overdue for payment.

   B: Well, no. I'm afraid it is already five weeks overdue.

5 A: The documents will be ready by Thursday as you requested.

   B: Sorry. It's on Tuesday that I need them.

6 A: So your office number is 064 735 458.

   B: No, 735 498.

🔊 **32 Listen to check your answers. Then listen again and take Speaker B's role.**

Project management

A **Complete the sentences with words from the box.**

> tender   resources   interpersonal   milestones   progress report
> risks   delegate   sponsor   ~~stakeholders~~   juggle

1 The people who have responsibility within a project and are likely to receive advantages from it are called the .*stakeholders*.......... .

2 Besides having a wide range of project management techniques at their fingertips, successful project managers also have the ability to set .... and targets.

3 If a project has a strong ...., i.e. someone who is ready to support it actively, then it is much more likely to succeed.

4 A..................... is a formal statement of the price you would charge for doing a job or providing goods or services.

5 To be a good project manager you need to know how to .... tasks to other people.

6 Regular meetings are important because they give everyone the opportunity to get a .... on what has been achieved so far.

7 .... include staff, particular knowledge or skills, money and time.

8 If you want to be a project manager, you need to be able to .... different issues all at the same time, i.e. to be good at multi-tasking.

9 Managing a project means working closely with other people, so obviously it's not something you can do unless you have excellent .... skills.

10 There are different ways to shorten delivery times but, whichever you use, make sure you assess the .... first.

B **Complete the words by writing in the missing letters.**

1 A successful project is one which is on time, on _u_ge_ and to performance.

2 Our company has decided that 10 per cent savings have to be made in all departments so we need to decide how best to make c_t_ _cks.

3 The Blake–Martins consortium has won a _i_ for the $1 billion Raghavan Port in Gujarat, western India.

4 In less than a year, the first phase of the project was already six months behind s_ _ _d_le.

5 Stakeholders sometimes ask for an earlier delivery date but without reducing the s_op_ of work.

6 Pr_cu_ _ _ _ _t is the act of ordering and buying the equipment, supplies and services needed by a company or organisation.

7 A Gantt _ _ _r_ shows the different stages of a project, the stages that can be done at the same time and those that have to be completed before others can begin.

8 The time when one can relax, delay a task but still finish the project on time is called _ _ _ck time.

C Complete each group of collocations with the correct keyword from the box.

a decision   results   a deadline   ~~a project~~   a goal   a team

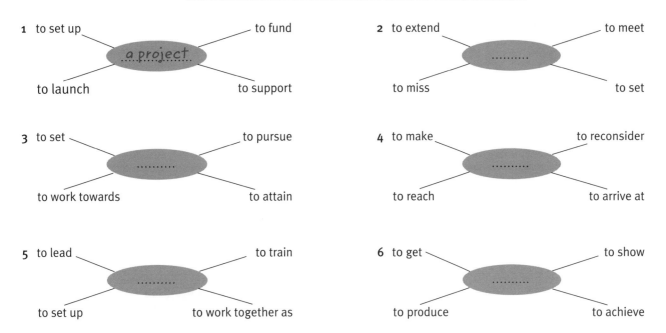

1 to set up / to launch — **a project** — to fund / to support

2 to extend / to miss — .... — to meet / to set

3 to set / to work towards — .... — to pursue / to attain

4 to make / to reach — .... — to reconsider / to arrive at

5 to lead / to set up — .... — to train / to work together as

6 to get / to produce — .... — to show / to achieve

D Match the sentence halves.

1 As the negotiations failed to produce results,

2 Some people say working with a 'virtual team' means

3 When you set up a project, make sure

4 You need excellent people skills

5 A good project manager should discuss issues with all members of the team

6 We asked our client to extend the deadline

a) there's no real sense of working towards a common goal.

b) because the second half of the funds was not forthcoming.

c) and then make decisions together with them.

d) in order to lead a team effectively.

e) we decided to call an emergency meeting.

f) you pick your team judiciously.

E Complete the sentences with suitable prepositions.

1 A successful project is .... time and .... budget.

2 Bad news: we are already 12 per cent .... budget and three weeks .... schedule.

3 A good project manager has to be good .... communicating so that people are aware .... what they are supposed to be doing.

4 Typically, the sponsor is involved .... setting the milestones .... the project.

5 We have been trying .... vain to get this project .... the ground .... weeks now.

A Indicate what the words in italics refer to.

Virtuoso Teams: Lessons from Teams that Changed their Worlds

By Andy Boynton and Bill Fischer (FT Prentice Hall)

In the case study hell of the business book world, the same corporate names keep cropping up: Dell, Southwest Airlines, Cemex, Swatch. But the opening pages of *this book*[1] contain the following unusual confession:

'We found lots of examples of virtuoso teams in the firms that we worked with, yet almost always *they*[2] were reluctant to tell their stories for publication because of modesty, internal politics and even jealousy.'

Not everyone will find *that explanation*[3] plausible. But let it go – for the moment. Because this alleged lack of cooperation has forced *the authors*[4] to cast their net wider and offer a range of examples that is far more inspiring than *those*[5] usually retold in books of this kind.

Andy Boynton, dean of the Carroll school of management in Boston, in the US, and Bill Fischer, professor of technology management at IMD in Lausanne, Switzerland, look to the arts, sciences and to the great 'Amundsen versus Scott' race to the South Pole to illustrate *their*[6] concept of the 'virtuoso team'. Only one actual business, Norsk Hydro, gets a look-in.

What a relief. And what a pleasure to read, for example, about the frenetic team of writers assembled by the NBC television network in the 1950s that was to create Sid Caesar's 'Your Show of Shows'.

B Complete the next part of the article with the reference words and phrases from the box.

| its   that   team   them   these individual all-stars   they |

.....................[1], containing such talent as Mel Brooks, Neil Simon, Woody Allen and Larry Gelbart, was packed with ability – and egos to match. It was 'like going to work every day of the week inside a Marx brothers movie', Gelbart observed. Ideas flew across the writers' room at a mercurial rate, jokes polished and perfected as ....[2] went along. Each week 90 minutes of new material was created, and got ....[3] only test-run live, on national television, in front of 20 million people.

But what made this a virtuoso team? Not just the talent but the way it was led. 'This was a team with incredible loyalty to its leader,' the authors say, 'not because ....[4] were predisposed to respect authority – quite the contrary – but because Sid Caesar paid ....[5] the ultimate professional compliment: he listened to them; he believed in them and he trusted them; over and over again.'

C **For each sentence, indicate in which of the underlined items there is a mistake, then write the correction in the table below.**

1 Klaus Kleinfeld, whom(a) in January 2005 took charge at Siemens, the German industrial group that is one of the world's(b) biggest manufacturers, is the 11th chief executive in the company's 158-year history and only the fifth not to be(c) related to Werner von Siemens, its founder.*

2 With his individualistic management style(a) and a furious pace of working that she expects(b) others to match, the 48-year-old has an approach at odds with the consensual style often associated with(c) German boardrooms.

3 While it has(a) managed to avoid some of the problems who have(b) brought other big European industrial groups to their knees in recent years, Siemens faces(c) a difficult economic background in Europe and tougher competition from rivals in low-cost countries.

4 Its operating profit margins, analysts point out(a), are only around half of that(b) achieved in the industrial activities of General Electric, the US company that(c) is a long-time rival to Siemens in many business segments.

5 In his first interview with a business publication since he took(a) the top job, Mr Kleinfeld emphasises a desire(b) to speed up innovation within the company and cut costs and hint that(c) businesses that continue to miss earnings targets could be jettisoned.

Sentence	Incorrect item	Correction
1	....	....
2	....	....
3	....	....
4	....	....
5	....	....

*Klaus Kleinfeld left Siemens in July 2007 to become chief executive of Alcoa.

D **Complete the second sentence in each pair so that it means approximately the same as the first sentence. Use between *three* and *seven* words, including the word given.**

1 The launch of the project was delayed by unforeseen problems with the sponsor. (**held**)

The launch of the project was ....
unexpected problems with the sponsor.

2 The project will go ahead as long as we manage to complete Phase 1 within budget. (**subject**)

The project will go ahead .... Phase 1 within budget.

3 The only thing we can do is wait for their progress report. (**anything**)

There .... wait for their progress report.

4 Relationships with the population affected by the project seem to be improving. (**signs**)

Relationships with the population affected by the project ....
....

5 Not as many people invest in projects of this kind now as ten years ago. (**lot**)

There are .... in projects of this kind now than ten years ago.

A 33 **The CEO of a large travel supplier is being interviewed about an invitation to tender the company issued recently. Listen and complete the text of the interview.**

Interviewer:	If I remember correctly, you issued your invitation to tender last December. What's been going on since?
CEO:	Well, the ..*closing*..[1] date for replies was exactly a week ago, March 31st that is. In those three months, 24 companies sent us their technical and ....[2] proposals in the areas of computer reservation system services and ....[3] applications.
Interviewer:	Twenty-four! Did you expect that many?
CEO:	In fact, it's a lot more than we expected ...
Interviewer:	Can you comment on the proposals at this stage?
CEO:	All we can say at this point is that we are extremely pleased with the ....[4] and ....[5] of all the proposals which we received. I repeat: all of them.
Interviewer:	So I assume you now have a tough task ahead?
CEO:	A tough one indeed! We've now got to start the ....[6] stage, as you might expect. We've already formed an Evaluation Committee, whose task will be to ....[7] all 24 proposals so they can analyse costs, seek functional demonstrations and meet key management staff of the companies that ....[8].
Interviewer:	How long will that take?
CEO:	We expect the whole ....[9] to take about two months.
Interviewer:	And then?
CEO:	If all goes well, we should be able to ....[10] contracts in the first half of June.
Interviewer:	Thank you very much for these details. We're all looking forward to the decisions of the Evaluation Committee.

B **Use the text of the interview in Exercise A to complete the press release below.**

As you write, make sure you:

- focus on key information
- leave out unnecessary details
- use an appropriate level of formality.

PRESS RELEASE

In an interview with our correspondent yesterday, Mary Sinding, CEO of Global Tours, announced that as many as 24 companies had replied to her RFP launched in December.

The proposals, which are in the areas of CRS services and Internet applications, ...

C Complete these sentences about teleconferencing with a suitable linker.

1 The chairperson should always take a roll call at the start. ...., he or she should outline the agenda and the objectives of the meeting.

2 .... it had all been made clear when we went over the basic rules, some of the participants did not respect the speaking time limit.

3 When I chair a teleconference, I always keep an eye on the clock. ...., it sometimes overruns.

4 When you chair a teleconference, make sure you pause periodically. So .... getting feedback, you can also take questions from the participants.

5 I shortened my final contribution .... the chairperson had time to go over the main points again.

D ◀)) 34 Listen to how certain sounds are linked together in these sentences.

1 I need to make‿a list‿of‿all‿attendees.

2 Let's decide‿on what‿options we'll use for‿our call.

> ### Explanation
> When a word ends with a consonant sound and the word immediately after begins with a vowel sound, we usually link those two words.

◀)) 34 Listen again and practise the sentences.

E ◀)) 35 Indicate where similar consonant–vowel links could be made in these sentences. Then listen to check your answers.

1 I'm afraid I haven't been able to create an agenda for the conference.

2 I don't like it when people bring up an issue which isn't on the agenda.

3 I contacted everyone and gave them the date and time of the teleconference.

4 I'd provided everyone with a lot of supplementary material well in advance.

5 It's always a nice addition to have some biographical information about the participants.

F Circle the word in each group which has a different stress pattern. Then check your answers in the Key.

Example: stakeholder criteria management

> ### Explanation
> We say *stakeholder* and *management* (stress on the first syllable) but *criteria* (stress on the second syllable).

1 successful	important	sensible
2 difficult	effective	external
3 resources	objective	consequence
4 overview	quality	decision
5 motivate	deliver	organise

◀)) 36 Listen and practise saying the words.

Answer key

1 First impressions

Word power

2 place emphasis on
3 made arrangements for
4 the best of my knowledge
5 us a brief summary
6 is scheduled for publication
7 a hasty conclusion
8 give me some guidance
9 a significant reduction in
10 as replacements for
11 (the) head of

The words which should be crossed out are:
2 a publicity
3 an accurate
4 a session
5 to arise
6 to delegate

2 a keynote speaker
3 a hostile audience
4 a pep talk
5 to fire questions
6 conference; held

2 a   3 b   4 c   5 a   6 b

Text and grammar

A

2 c   3 e   4 a   5 h   6 f

B

It may sometimes be possible to place the adverb in a different place. The sentences below are from the original article.
1 they also <u>actively</u> seek to reinforce them
2 you have to work so much harder <u>afterwards</u>
3 you need to ensure you are <u>physically</u> relaxed
4 Don't put yourself in a position where you're <u>forever</u> having to cover up
5 do not take mobile phone calls unless you <u>absolutely</u> have to
6 What if things are going <u>badly</u>?
7 I had a client who had a job interview with a chief executive who <u>barely</u> looked at him.
8 After that, the interview <u>actually</u> went okay and he got the job.

Skills and pronunciation

A

2 f   3 a   4 c   5 b   6 e

B

1 We are writing to inform you
2 We realise this is a topic close to your own heart
3 We would be honoured
4 attend the event
5 We would be extremely grateful
6 if you could confirm your talk at your earliest convenience
7 Please do not hesitate to contact me
8 should you require further details
9 With best wishes

C

The first sentence in each pair is a neutral statement, while the second one has a much more dramatic effect. The second structure is often used in written communications and in oral presentations to create an **impact,** or to highlight a **contrast** with something that was previously written or said. For example: *Downsizing will lead us nowhere. What we need is a radical management shake-up.*

D

1 What I'm looking forward to is a good networking function. / It's a good networking function (that) I'm looking forward to.
2 What they don't like is slang or colloquialisms. / It's slang or colloquialisms (that) they don't like.
3 What matters most is your rapport with the audience. / It's your rapport with the audience that matters most.
4 What I didn't like was the sort of questions they asked me. / It's (*or* It was) the sort of questions they asked me (that) I didn't like.
5 What they expect is a high-tech presentation. / It's a high-tech presentation (that) they expect.

E

Speaker 1: f
Speaker 2: b
Speaker 3: d
Speaker 4: b
Speaker 5: d
Speaker 6: a
Speaker 7: f
Speaker 8: a

F *See audio script 3.*

2 Training

Word power

 A

2 d   3 c   4 a   5 f   6 e

 B

2 vocational training
3 performance appraisal
4 work placement
5 human resources
6 team building

C

The words which should be crossed out are:
2 tuition
3 to educate one's
4 to enter
5 qualification
6 to fulfil

D

2 Life-long learning
3 embarking on a career
4 has run; course
5 Assertiveness training
6 create; posts

E

Across		Down	
2	rejig	1	pejorative
3	send	4	exposed
6	hone	5	dots
7	spot		
8	track		
9	divorced		
10	versatile		

F

2 feedback
3 role
4 graduates
5 employers
6 choice
7 skilled

Text and grammar

 A

2 had begun (*or* began)
3 would be leaving (*or* was leaving)
4 discovered
5 tended
6 will be leaving
7 developed
8 studied
9 accepted
10 returned
11 was
12 realised
13 made
14 had only included

B

1 (in); at
2 for; of; to
3 for; at
4 on; per
5 of; in; on
6 on; for; about
7 from; to
8 between; for
9 in; in
10 from

C

2	each	7	to
3	of	8	In
4	at	9	so
5	such	10	a
6	has		

D

3 with
4 for
5 ✓
6 either
7 and
8 the
9 even
10 ✓
11 about
12 or
13 a
14 ✓

Skills and pronunciation

■ Sample answer

… The workshop was facilitated by Dennis Pierce of Nexus Business Consultancy. Mr Pierce is a world-renowned expert in his field and this particular workshop certainly exceeded all the participants' expectations.

One of the aims of the workshop was to provide us with a set of tips and techniques to express our rights, requests, opinions and feelings honestly, directly and appropriately. In addition, we had ample opportunity to practise those techniques through role play and team work.

This has raised my awareness of the importance of building positive relationships, while it has also boosted my confidence when difficult decisions need to be taken. If there is one thing about this workshop I am not happy about, it is only the fact that nobody else from the Design Department was able to attend. I would strongly recommend that in future such workshops should not be scheduled in the period January to March, when Design is often at its busiest. Next year, I would find it particularly useful to attend a computer skills course focusing on the X-tron software package. I have no doubt that other people in Design would find such a course useful, too. Indeed, since we adopted this new software six months ago, we have experienced many difficulties. A hands-on course should enable us to use this state-of-the-art software to its full potential.

Speaker 1: c
Speaker 2: a
Speaker 3: d
Speaker 4: b
Speaker 5: e

1 Speaker 2
2 Speaker 5
3 Speaker 1
4 Speaker 3
5 Speaker 4

 See audio script 6.

 See audio script 8.

3 Energy

Word power

2 worth
3 cost
4 expand
5 come

2 a 3 d 4 f 5 c 6 e

2 carbon emissions
3 tidal power
4 wind turbines
5 solar panels
6 renewable energies

1 stifle
2 move
3 deny
4 curb
5 wean

2 promotion
3 speculative
4 stability
5 growth
6 production
7 expansion
8 expectations
9 industrial
10 credibility
11 likely
12 strength
13 cyclical
14 performance

Text and grammar

2 The
3 ∅
4 the
5 a
6 ∅
7 the
8 the
9 ∅
10 the
11 ∅
12 the
13 ∅
14 the
15 the
16 ∅
17 ∅

<u>A</u> key question is whether nuclear energy would be economically viable. The upfront costs are discouragingly high at <u>an</u> estimated $1,300 to $1,500 per kilowatt to build <u>a</u> nuclear plant, which works out as roughly twice what it costs to build <u>a</u> gas-fired power station. However, proponents claim that over the life of <u>a</u> nuclear plant, it can generate energy at <u>a</u> cost comparable to or even cheaper than that of conventional fossil-fuel power.

2 b 3 e 4 g 5 f 6 a 7 c

2 in
3 for
4 about
5 against
6 to
7 under
8 into
9 for
10 on
11 to

3 there
4 ✓
5 an
6 ✓
7 too
8 the
9 at
10 any
11 his
12 ✓
13 over
14 a

Skills and pronunciation

2 despite
3 in order to
4 thus
5 unless
6 however
7 Given

Sample answer

The aim of this report is to summarise the changes in the transport infrastructure budget for the period between 2006 and 2010. We shall also focus on the trends in budget allocation between railways and roads.

Railway investment declined steadily from €400m in 2006 to €200m in 2008. It remained at the same level the next year but then climbed sharply to reach €500m in 2010.

Road investment, by contrast, rose steadily from €500m to €800m in the first three years. It fell by €300m in 2009, before peaking at €1.1bn in 2010.

Finally, the chart shows clearly that a larger part of the budget was consistently allocated to roads. Although the difference was only slight in 2006, the budget apportioned to roads in the next four years was always at least twice as big as the budget for the development of the railway infrastructure.

Sample answers

1 sufficient daylight (or enough daylight)
2 thousands of euros
3 an excellent investment
4 ventilation and cooling
5 at least half
6 periodic maintenance
7 extremely cost-effective
8 15
9 two-thirds
10 peak demand period
11 periods of inactivity
12 40 per cent

 See audio script 10.

4 Marketing

Word power

2 mailshots
3 Cold calling
4 relationship management
5 Door-to-door
6 catalogues
7 social media
8 text messaging
9 Word-of-mouth
10 e-mails

1 consumer
2 launched
3 run
4 cost
5 target

2 d   3 e   4 c   5 f   6 a

2 earnings gap
3 mass market
4 viral marketing
5 customer loyalty
6 market share

The following words should be crossed out:
2 loan
3 trade
4 venture
5 balance
6 account
7 production
8 expense

Text and grammar

The following should be crossed out:
2 ∅ *and* who
3 who *and* that
4 that *and* whom
5 that *and* which
6 ∅ *and* which
7 who *and* whose
8 ∅ *and* who

And if, as Kotler argues, customers are the new brand owners, it's clear that their values will significantly influence those brands. Companies <u>that (*or* which)</u> 'get' the 3.0 model, he says, will integrate the right values into every aspect of their business and then market that mission to their audience. 'The company wants to live out a set of values and these values give the company its personality and purpose,' Kotler says.

Kotler even draws comparisons between Marketing 3.0 and the agenda outlined in the United Nations Millennium Development Goals of 2000, <u>which</u> endorsed efforts to eradicate poverty and hunger, advance universal primary education and reduce child mortality. Profit will result when consumers appreciate a company's efforts to improve human well-being – whether that is The Walt Disney Company working to address wellness issues facing children or S.C. Johnson & Son's positioning as a sustainable family business <u>that (*or* which)</u> serves millions of people living on less than $1 a day.

Marketing 3.0 is selling hope along with the soap, touching people's hearts and minds. It's a transformation, says Kotler, <u>whose</u> time has come.

2 that were withdrawn
3 that regard advertising
4 that was postponed
5 that is
6 that were left
7 that we launched
8 that they recalled
9 that we hired
10 that Tim left
11 that marketing gurus
12 that I met

1 who
2 which
3 who
4 which
5 who
6 which
7 which / ∅
8 which / ∅
9 who(m)* / ∅
10 which / ∅
11 which / ∅
12 who(m)* / ∅

* In formal English, we often use *whom* instead of *who* as the object of the verb in the relative clause, especially in writing.

2 why
3 whose
4 where
5 when
6 where

Skills and pronunciation

2 plan
3 cut
4 increase
5 start
6 stopped
7 launched
8 decided
9 credit
10 ask
11 sum up
12 recognise

 Sample answer

Reducing advertising costs
➢ social networking
➢ word-of-mouth referrals
➢ blogs

Speaker 1: f
Speaker 2: b
Speaker 3: d
Speaker 4: b
Speaker 5: a
Speaker 6: f
Speaker 7: e
Speaker 8: c

 Sample answers

1 Executives in their 30s and under grew up with an IT infrastructure, e-mail and the internet; they are the so-called 'digital natives'. But people in the 50s age group were only exposed to new technologies later in their career so they have a lot to catch up with.
2 Young people and all those consumers who decide what to buy on the basis of discussions in the social media space.
3 Unhappy customers don't hesitate to vent their frustrations on social media channels.
4 Because employees might misuse social media, which could lead to marketing damage.
5 Because they can familiarise older executives with the new technologies.

1 are at a disadvantage
2 risk missing out on
3 can't respond to
4 implement guidelines for; result in
5 understanding; value; revenue generators

The following words should be circled:
1 reward
2 manage
3 answer
4 effective
5 consumer
6 company

5 Employment trends

Word power

2 Migrant
3 self-employed
4 turnover
5 seasonal
6 shift
7 security
8 absenteeism
9 portfolio
10 bonus

1 (terminate*)
2 dismiss*
3 take on
4 lay off
5 select
6 leave*

*although *end /terminate*, *fire /dismiss*, *quit /leave* are synonyms, they are different in style; *end*, *fire* and *quit* are much more informal than *terminate*, *dismiss* and *leave*.

2 h   3 e   4 f   5 b   6 g   7 d   8 a

2 redundancy package
3 attrition rates
4 communication skills
5 human resources
6 Job security
7 maternity leave
8 work-life balance

2 build
3 labour
4 earned
5 record
6 getting

Text and grammar

2 to say
3 to give up; working
4 to find; doing
5 to be; handing in
6 to meet; losing
7 doing; to go back
8 to express

2 d   3 c   4 e   5 h   6 b

3 in
4 of
5 ✓
6 under
7 in
8 ✓
9 in
10 many
11 they
12 no
13 if
14 ✓
15 ✓

Skills and pronunciation

2 a   3 f   4 h   5 d   6 e   7 b   8 c

1 contrast
2 noun
3 verb
4 of
5 stronger

Sample answers

2 Staff morale is relatively good even though they have to deal with a lot of abusive calls.
   Despite having to deal with a lot of abusive calls, staff morale is relatively good.
3 Even though he had been promised promotion, he decided to hand in his notice.
   He decided to hand in his notice in spite of having been promised promotion.
4 Employee loyalty was good although working conditions were appalling.
   In spite of the appalling working conditions, employee loyalty was good.
5 Although the company has a formal grievance procedure, staff hardly ever voice their complaints.
   Staff hardly ever voice their complaints even though the company has a formal grievance procedure.
6 They failed to find a mutually acceptable solution although they were both quite flexible.
   Even though they were both quite flexible, they failed to find a mutually acceptable solution.

Sample answer

The aim of this report is to describe the movements in employment levels in the manufacturing and service industries in a particular capital city and country in the period 2004–2010.
As regards the manufacturing industry, the level of employment in the capital dropped significantly until 2007, even more so than in the country as a whole. There was a 20 per cent and a 15 per cent fall in the capital and in the country respectively. However, employment in the city rose dramatically by 15 per cent until mid 2009, and then began falling again until the end of 2010. By contrast, the national employment level rose steadily by 15 per cent from early 2008 till 2010.
As to the service industry, levels of employment rose by over 25 per cent in the capital and in the country as a whole. This increase happened very steadily at the national level but with several fluctuations in the capital city where, for example, a sharp increase from mid 2006 till the end of 2007 was followed by a rapid fall in 2008. From mid 2009, however, employment levels in the services have shown a clear upward trend in the capital.

There are five mistakes altogether. *See audio script 14.*

The following words should be circled:
1 abusive
2 atmosphere
3 motivation
4 location

6 Ethics

Word power

2 Accountability
3 Fraudulent
4 Sustainability
5 whistleblower
6 supply chain
7 stakeholders
8 Nepotism
9 Wrongdoing

1 Fairtrade
2 Accountability
3 fraudulent
4 nepotism
5 stakeholders

2 illegal
3 immoral
4 dishonest
5 unconvincing
6 irresponsible
7 unethical
8 imprudent
9 unaccountable
10 indirect

1 lawsuit
2 legitimate
3 illegally; legalised
4 lawfully
5 lawyer
6 legitimise

2 effectiveness
3 employees
4 guidance
5 judgment (or judgement)
6 investigative
7 disciplinary
8 violation
9 relationships
10 acceptable
11 pressure
12 compliance
13 growth

Text and grammar

A

1 (can't); must
2 shouldn't
3 should
4 wouldn't
5 should
6 needn't
7 may not (or might not)
8 should

B

2 b   3 a   4 b   5 a   6 c

C

2 matter how enthusiastic
3 unless we set up
4 not nearly as good as
5 to blame our suppliers for
6 to stamp out
7 for the CEO admitting
8 drew the board's attention to
9 so impatient that he did
10 suggest we (or suggest that we should or suggest we should or suggest that we)
11 look forward to (or are looking forward to)

Skills and pronunciation

Sample answer

The aim of this report is first of all to set out the rationale for a Code of Conduct (subsequently referred to as 'Code'). I shall then proceed to recommend a number of key areas which, in my experience, ought to be covered in our future Code.

Although so far we have not had grounds to complain about the conduct of any of our employees, our rapid expansion in a number of other countries means that we increasingly have to rely on individuals from diverse backgrounds who are scarcely acquainted with our values and principles. The aim of such a Code is to inform our employees of our values and expectations.

As we are essentially a service organisation, it is essential that our employees perform their duties in a manner that maintains and enhances public confidence and trust in our integrity. Our employees are our most valuable asset and we must therefore enable every one of them to demonstrate the highest standards of behaviour.

Finally, with regard to the areas that should be covered in the Code, I would like at this stage to make four recommendations.

1. Professionalism: This could include dress code, courtesy towards clients and use of appropriate language.
2. Harassment: We are an equal opportunities employer and as such we cannot tolerate any form of behaviour which could cause the work environment to be stressful or discriminatory for some employees.
3. Use of the organisation's property and equipment
4. Moonlighting

B

Speaker 1: f
Speaker 2: b
Speaker 3: f
Speaker 4: a
Speaker 5: d
Speaker 6: a
Speaker 7: d
Speaker 8: b

1 c   2 c   3 a   4 a   5 b   6 a   7 b   8 b

ANSWER KEY

7 Finance

Word power

 A

2 c	3 b	4 a	5 a	6 b	7 c	8 b	9 b
10 a	11 c	12 c	13 a	14 b	15 b		

B

2 e	3 a	4 c	5 g	6 b	7 f

C

2 a	3 d	4 f	5 g	6 c	7 b	8 e

2 bridging loan
3 tax evasion
4 debt funding
5 overdraft facilities
6 business angel
7 pension fund
8 savings account

2 consumers
3 savings
4 proportion
5 advisers
6 erosion

Text and grammar

A

1 a) brought down
  b) bring down
  c) bring down
2 a) get away
  b) got away
  c) get away
3 a) giving away
  b) give away
  c) gave (him) away
4 a) to take off (*or* taking off)
  b) took off
  c) take (my shirt) off
5 a) turned (it) down
  b) turn (the TV) down
  c) turn down

B

2 a	3 c	4 a	5 c	6 b	7 c	8 a

2 will be
3 follows
4 are
5 is being implemented
6 has improved
7 made
8 grown
9 achieved
10 have improved

Our strategy for Bentix is to position the brand as a major player in the medium cost health and personal care arena, by not only expanding its antiseptics offering, but also diversifying into other health care products. Earlier this year we started testing essential oils and herbal remedies with some success and we will look to introduce more new product concepts over the next 12 to 18 months. We will be deploying many of the successful initiatives tested in the first half before the festive season.

Skills and pronunciation

 Sample answer

The chart shows the trends in banking concentration in five countries over the decade 2001–2010. The top five banks significantly increased their market share in all countries except Japan, where there was a slight decrease from 32 to 29 per cent.

The most remarkable increase in concentration occurred in Sweden, where the top five banks controlled 85 per cent of the market in 2010 against 62 per cent in 2001. In the Netherlands too, the top five controlled over 80 per cent of the market at the end of the period under consideration, which represents an increase of nearly 10 per cent.

Finally, the market share of the top five in Germany and Italy increased from 16 to 18 and from 25 to 38 per cent respectively in the ten-year period.

B

1 returns	6 buyback
2 revenues	7 interim
3 income	8 final
4 surplus	9 approved
5 dividend	10 repurchased

1 F	2 T	3 F	4 T	5 T	6 F	7 F

 Sample answers

1 Because this sector often needs a lot of capital in the early stages, for example for testing and experimenting.
2 The green plug is an environment-friendly product because it helps save energy.
3 They approached banks and also applied for government loans.
4 Business angels and family and friends
5 Saving energy and resources

1 came up with; turn off; switched on
2 could do with
3 turned down
4 cut in on
5 turn to; deal with

1 cut in on	5 come up with
2 could do with	6 deal with
3 turn off	7 turn down
4 turn to	8 switch on

8 Consultants

Word power

2 a 3 b 4 b 5 a 6 c 7 a 8 c 9 b
10 b 11 c 12 a

B

2 plan out
3 pack up
4 go through
5 circle back
6 wrap up
7 hammer out
8 leave out

2 liabilities
3 independent
4 requirements
5 complexity
6 powerful
7 disagrees
8 exception
9 conscientious
10 proliferation

Text and grammar

■ Sample answers

2 Yes, I have.
3 Nine thirty.
4 Yes, I'd love to. Anywhere in mind?
5 Well, Svetlana should.
6 I have done already.
7 No idea.
8 I hope so.

■ Sample answers

2 If they had the necessary skills to do the work in-house, they wouldn't have to rely on an outside expert.
3 If I had been better prepared, I would feel good about the negotiation.
4 If he was (or were) a good communicator, we could ask him to conduct the negotiation.
5 If they had set a realistic timescale, the project would have been completed on time.
6 I wish I had been able to negotiate better terms.
7 If we had brought in a consultant, the crisis would have been defused more quickly.
8 If he wasn't (or weren't) an inefficient manager, his projects would be on budget.
9 If I had realised my client was dissatisfied, I would have made a substantial concession.
10 If we had been clear about what we wanted, we would be pleased with what we've got.

2 Should you be
3 unless we get
4 As long as
5 in case you

Skills and pronunciation

2 and then
3 Let's
4 I'm afraid this
5 In addition
6 However
7 But of course
8 Looking forward

B

Speaker 1: d
Speaker 2: c
Speaker 3: b
Speaker 4: f
Speaker 5: g

Speaker 1: c
Speaker 2: d
Speaker 3: e
Speaker 4: g
Speaker 5: a

■ *See audio script 24.*

1 I'd (*I would*); I were
2 I'd (*I had*) been; I'd (*I would*) have
3 might've (*might have*) been; we'd (*we had*)
4 we'll (*we will*) be; we
5 he'd (*he had*) been; he'd (*he would*) have been
6 they're (*they are*); they'll (*they will*)

9 Strategy

Word power

2 rate
3 range
4 accounts
5 hold
6 spending
7 reach
8 change
9 debt

B

2 staff turnover
3 competitive advantage
4 strategic planning
5 economic outlook
6 customer care
7 mission statement

C

2 added
3 increased
4 strengthened
5 remained
6 issued
7 implemented
8 named

Text and grammar

2 (b) each of whom
3 (c) being fine-tuned
4 (b) arguing that
5 (d) is expected
6 (b) to the enterprise

B

2 not be brought up
3 face up to the fact (or face the fact)
4 is the manager's responsibility
5 twice as many men
6 is not nearly as effective
7 went according to plan
8 planning is essential to
9 only I had taken
10 (high) time our currency was

C

3 up
4 to
5 ✓
6 early
7 the
8 very
9 a
10 and
11 ✓
12 to
13 if

Skills and pronunciation

1 strives to be the global leader
2 of advancing and applying
3 to offer
4 make the most of
5 helping individuals, businesses and communities
6 considers the environment

B

2 c   3 b   4 b   5 c   6 a   7 a   8 c

D *See audio script 27.*

F *See audio script 29.*

10 Online business

Word power

A

Across

1 social
3 Navigation
7 dotcom
8 Software

Down

1 search
2 click
4 tweet
5 stored
6 blog

B

2 c   3 b   4 c   5 a   6 b   7 b   8 c   9 a   10 c

C

2 f   3 e   4 b   5 a   6 d

Text and grammar

1 (a) still lack confidence
2 (c) it also results
3 (a) have their reasons
4 (b) during (or in) the last 15 years

B

2 is
3 and
4 of
5 who
6 if
7 from
8 to
9 an
10 that

1 f   2 d   3 c   4 a   5 e

Skills and pronunciation

A Sample answer

The aim of this report is to summarise the changes in the proportion of households with Internet access in France, Germany, Sweden and the UK between 2007 and 2009.
In 2007, Sweden was in the lead, with over three-quarters of households having access to the Internet. In second position came Germany, with 71 per cent, followed by the UK (67 per cent) and France (49 per cent).
By 2009, the four countries under scrutiny still occupied the same positions, but the percentage of households with Internet access had risen noticeably, most particularly in France, where a 14 per cent increase was recorded, and in the UK, with a 10 per cent increase. In Germany and in Sweden, the figure increased by 8 and 7 per cent respectively.

B

2 f   3 g   4 b   5 a   6 e   7 c   8 i   9 h

C

1 c   2 b   3 a   4 a   5 b   6 c

11 New business

Word power

1 Entrepreneurship
2 seed capital
3 pitch
4 grant
5 cash flow
6 Perseverance
7 business venture
8 differentiate
9 prototype
10 delivery

B

2 show
3 volume
4 vessel
5 fair
6 recall
7 reception
8 significant
9 mature
10 pay

2 a 3 d 4 d 5 c 6 b

Text and grammar

2 g 3 f 4 c 5 h 6 e 7 d 8 a

 Sample answers

3 It was Turkish Airlines that placed an order with Airbus for 20 new planes.
4 It was in 2009 that Turkish Airlines placed their order.
5 It was Airbus that Turkish Airlines placed their order with.
6 It was an order for 20 new planes that they placed.

2 difference
3 decision
4 solution
5 damage
6 difficulty

1 to (or towards)
2 to
3 in
4 for
5 to
6 on

3 them
4 ✓
5 the
6 and
7 such
8 it
9 ✓
10 down
11 much
12 about
13 an
14 ✓
15 them
16 it

Skills and pronunciation

2 f 3 e 4 d 5 c 6 h 7 b 8 g

Sample answer

With reference to your letter of 17 May, we would like to apologise for the delay in settling invoice No. P5K/200 and also for failing to reply to your first reminder.

The latter incident is the result of an oversight from our new administrative assistant, who has not yet got the hang of our accounts or filing systems.

On the other hand we must bear full responsibility for not settling the above-mentioned invoice in time. We were expecting one of our main suppliers to clear his balance with us by mid April. As he failed to do so until 15 May, it was extremely difficult for us to pay our suppliers.

However, we are pleased to inform you that our bank was given instructions yesterday to credit your account with £1,250.

Once again, please accept our apologies for this unfortunate concurrence of events. You can rest assured that we will do our utmost to avoid such delays in future. We look forward to doing further business with you.

Yours sincerely,

E. Lonza

E. Lonza
Purchasing Manager

D *See audio script 32.*

12 Project management

Word power

2 milestones
3 sponsor
4 tender
5 delegate
6 progress report
7 Resources
8 juggle
9 interpersonal
10 risks

B

1 budget
2 cutbacks
3 bid
4 schedule
5 scope
6 Procurement
7 chart
8 slack

2 a deadline
3 a goal
4 a decision
5 a team
6 results

D

2 a   3 f   4 d   5 c   6 b

E

1 on; within (or on)
2 over; behind
3 at; of
4 in; of (or for)
5 in; off; for

Text and grammar

2 *they* refers back to *virtuoso teams* (line 9)
3 *that explanation* refers back to people not telling their stories for publication *because of modesty, internal politics and even jealousy* (lines 12–14)
4 *the authors* refers back to Boynton and Fischer (*see title*)
5 *those* refers back to *examples* (line 21)
6 *their* refers back to Boynton and Fischer (lines 24–29)

B

1 That team
2 they
3 its
4 these individual all-stars
5 them

1 (a) Klaus Kleinfeld, who
2 (b) he expects
3 (b) the problems that have (or which have)
4 (b) half of those
5 (c) and hints that

D

1 held up by (or held up due to)
2 subject to our completing (or subject to the completion of)
3 isn't anything we can do other than (or isn't anything we can do except)
4 show signs of improvement (or show signs of improving)
5 a lot fewer people who invest (or a lot fewer people investing)

Skills and pronunciation

2 cost
3 Internet
4 content
5 quality
6 evaluation
7 review
8 bid
9 process
10 award

Sample answer

In an interview with our correspondent yesterday, Mary Sinding, CEO of Global Tours, announced that as many as 24 companies had replied to her RFP launched in December. The proposals, which are in the areas of CRS services and Internet applications, are all of excellent quality, the CEO added.
The Evaluation Committee, which has already been established, now faces the difficult task of evaluating the offers for functional suitability and cost effectiveness. According to Ms Sinding, the evaluation process should take approximately two months and contracts should be awarded by mid June.

1 In addition
2 Although (or Though or Even though)
3 However (or Even so)
4 besides (or as well as or in addition to)
5 so that

E   *See audio script 35.*

F

The following words should be circled:
1 sensible
2 difficult
3 consequence
4 decision
5 deliver

Audio scripts

1 First impressions

1

Speaker 1: I'd like to bring this short presentation to a close now and get some feedback from you on the main issues that have been dealt with.

Speaker 2: It's clear that we have dramatically increased our shareholdings in the main regional operators. Moving on to the area of international partnerships, I would now like to give you the latest details of our SMW4 cable system project.

Speaker 3: Now, if we turn our attention for a moment to this graph here on the flip chart, we can see quite clearly a slight upward trend in profit figures over the past six months.

Speaker 4: So I take it that all of us now understand the rationale for the cost-cutting measures we're proposing. The next point I'd like to consider is the strategy we'll adopt to implement those measures.

Speaker 5: The figures speak for themselves. If you look at the table in the bottom right-hand corner of your handout, you'll see that the situation is far from being as bad as some people would have us believe.

Speaker 6: The purpose of this presentation is to provide an overview of the European car market over the past five years and to outline what I see as the necessary conditions for its recovery.

Speaker 7: Well, I think we've covered a lot of ground this morning. I'd like to round off my talk now with a brief recap of the main points.

Speaker 8: Today, I'd like to talk about outsourcing in general and the potential benefits of outsourcing for our company in particular.

2

1 Pleased to meet you.
2 Our website's just been updated.
3 Sorry, I didn't quite catch your last point.

3

1 It's hard to say which aspects are the most positive.
2 The second talk focused particularly on deregulation.
3 Last summer we worked together on a research project.
4 The first presentation wasn't very difficult to understand.
5 I wouldn't say it was the greatest networking event I've ever attended.

2 Training

4

Speaker 1: I think I've always been realistic when setting the goals for the year ahead so, as a result, I can't really say I've failed to achieve any. I've consistently met my sales targets, although the third quarter was really borderline. Relationships with our distributors have improved considerably. That was hard work but I got there in the end. Taking responsibility for my own professional development, yes, definitely. I took the course on energy saving at work and I've already signed up for the next one, on conflict resolution.

Speaker 2: My post has always offered a lot of variety, of course, with some aspects of it becoming more important at certain times or moving into the background at other times. Having said that, since my last performance review, I've had roughly the same responsibilities. So I would tend to say that it's still appropriate, although since January I've also been responsible for the training of some new staff members. And I'm glad to hear I'll be doing a lot more of that in the future. On the other hand, I no longer have to contribute to our newsletter as it's been discontinued so we need to take that out. And if we put in induction, then it'll be much more accurate.

Speaker 3: My job involves working with people all the time, listening to their worries, advising, comforting, suggesting possible courses of action, etc. Most people are really grateful just to have found a sympathetic ear, someone who helps them iron out the difficulties they encounter at work, and that's great. But there are also those who come back to you after a while, almost wagging an angry finger at you, saying I tried this, I tried that, it didn't work, in fact it failed miserably and it was all your idea. It's tough when you feel you're being got at. I don't think I'll ever be able to cope with that.

Speaker 4: My priority was, of course, to try to meet the objectives we'd agreed on last year. But, apart from that, I really appreciate the fact that I had opportunities to develop some new skills. For example, I took over the organisation of our third regional conference and I also volunteered to write the proceedings. It's not something I'd want to do every year but someone had to do it and I acquitted myself quite well on the task. I also reshuffled the marketing team a bit and I'm rather proud of the fact that they seem much happier to work together now.

Speaker 5: Well, on the whole, I'm generally happy with the quality of the work I produce and so are our clients. I don't want to sound self-satisfied but I really think it'd be difficult to produce anything that's significantly better. I keep trying, of course! One area I think calls for improvement is meeting deadlines. Not that I often miss them but it's a lot of stress always working to tight deadlines. What I need to work on is managing my time more effectively so I no longer have to work flat out till the minute an important order is due for collection.

5

1 We all agree the previous course was a lot easier.
2 The information I get is often out of date.

6

1 Let's talk about it in more detail.
2 Those courses are always intensive.
3 First of all, I just analyse the company's needs.
4 She's been acting as a coach for a company director.
5 A mentor is often someone who has a lot of experience.

7

1 A: So we all meet again on the 30th. Is that right?
  B: Sorry, no. Our next meeting is on the <u>13th</u>.
2 A: Can I just check the first name, please? Is that F-R-A-N-C-I-S?
  B: C-<u>E</u>-S. F-R-A-N-C-<u>E</u>-S. Mrs Frances Potter.

8

1 A: Let me just check that. First, the Leadership Skills course starts next Tuesday.
  B: Not quite. It starts on <u>Thurs</u>day.
2 A: ... and if I understood you correctly, the Leadership Skills course is free of charge.
  B: Sorry, no. It's the <u>Computer</u> Skills course that's free of charge.
3 A: Did you say the seminar room is on the first floor?
  B: No, it's on the <u>third</u> floor, actually.
4 A: The number of participants has now increased to 25.
  B: To <u>29</u>! And we're expecting even more.
5 A: So you graduated from the University of Chester.
  B: <u>Leicester</u>, actually. I graduated from the University of <u>Leicester</u> in 2008.
6 A: ... and the freelance trainer is Jeremy Langford. L-A-N-G- ...
  B: Sorry, that's spelt L-A-N-<u>K</u>-F-O-R-D.

3 Energy

9

Good morning, Ladies and Gentlemen, my name's Yasmina Jaziri-Gales. As you know, I'm from the Smart Energy Centre, where I work in a team of energy advisers to business managers. In my talk today, I'd simply like to report on the most common areas where we have noticed energy could easily be used more efficiently. After that, I'll outline a number of long-term solutions.

Let's start then with our most visible energy wasters. Although most of us are well aware of them, it seems that we don't really know what to do about them. All the reports for the seventy-odd companies we've worked with so far point in the same direction: the most costly waste of energy occurs in three areas: lighting, heating and office equipment. Let's consider each area in turn. As a rule, if there is sufficient daylight, turn off fluorescent lights. It sounds simple, my grandmother certainly believed in this rule, yet unnecessary use of fluorescent light costs companies thousands of euros every year. In addition, make a point of turning off the light whenever you are the last person to leave a room. Naturally, you can also make an excellent investment by installing dimmers and motion sensors.

I'd like to move on to my second point now, heating, and consider at the same time two closely related areas, ventilation and cooling. Did you know that space conditioning uses at least half the energy consumed in company buildings? It is therefore a prime target for major energy savings, much of which can be achieved at little cost. When it comes to reducing electricity consumption and extending the life of your equipment, periodic maintenance is the key. And you don't even need to call an expert to clean or replace air filters or to check pipe insulation for damage. Detailed maintenance instructions can be found in the equipment manuals. Another simple method is to ensure that all doors and windows are closed when the air conditioning or heating system is operating. It's good to hear some of you giggle, I thought you would, yet you'd be surprised. One audit after another shows that this is simply not put into practice as often as it should be. A useful additional strategy is to make sure that all doors and windows close tightly and to watch out for leaks, as minimising air infiltration can effectively reduce energy waste. Finally, make sure thermostats are set properly. A sound investment here would be to install programmable thermostats. They may be rather expensive but they are extremely cost-effective.

Now, on to our third point, office equipment. A simple and effective way to reduce energy use and costs is to turn the computer off when you leave the office for more than 15 minutes. Sometimes, the computer has to be left on continuously for network services or remote access, but even in these cases, the monitor can safely be turned off. You'll be interested to know that the monitor typically consumes two-thirds of the total energy used by the system. Many computers come with free software that automatically places active monitors into a low-power sleep mode through the local area network.

We may be dreaming of the paperless office but it is a fact that all the companies where we have carried out an audit have at least three photocopiers. A simple and useful tip here is to encourage staff not to use copiers during the peak demand period. In addition, ensure that the power saver switch on the copiers is enabled. Many copiers today are equipped with automatic controls to reduce their power consumption during periods of inactivity and to switch off the power after a further elapsed time interval. A copier with this simple feature can save you up to 40 per cent in electricity compared to standard models. Now then, before I take your questions, I'd just like to briefly outline a number of long-term solutions.

10

1 I'm not so *sure* I agree with you there.
2 I see things a little *differently* from you.
3 I *do* think it's important to act quickly.
4 We *just* can't afford to let the competition act first.
5 I know I keep *going* on about this, but it's our reputation that's at stake.
6 Let's not *make* any hasty decisions.
7 Let's *keep* our options open.
8 We should *think* this through a bit more.
9 I'm in two *minds* about it really.

4 Marketing

11

Speaker 1: So what I'd like you to think about in the next few days is what you yourself can do to improve communication with your customers.
Speaker 2: Now, in my opinion, what the marketing department really need to ask themselves is: How is consumer behaviour changing?
Speaker 3: What we need is a *global* vision for the future, not a medley of disparate ideas.
Speaker 4: How has the Internet changed our relationships with consumers?
Speaker 5: The solution is simple: listen to your customers, listen to what they need, listen to what they want, listen to what they are trying to tell you.

Speaker 6: If there's just one thing I'd like you all to remember, it's this: in the age of social networking, we can no longer rely on 19th-century advertising techniques.

Speaker 7: One of the things they taught me at school was to keep my opinions to myself. Now, I'm sure that's not your idea of education, is it?

Speaker 8: Let's not forget the words of the great Peter Drucker: the aim of marketing is to make selling unnecessary.

12

What's an RSS feed? What's cloud computing? What's a Twitter hashtag?

This may be a bit of a stereotype but if you're a business executive over the age of 50, the chances are that you won't know.

We're all aware that we are in the midst of a generational change. Executives in their 30s and under, the so-called digital natives, grew up with an IT infrastructure, e-mail and the Internet. On the other hand, those in the 50s age group are at a disadvantage because they were exposed later in their careers to learning new technologies. As a result, they may risk missing out on opportunities: for example, capturing new segments of the marketplace, particularly young people, as well as more generally the growing percentage of consumers who decide what to buy on the basis of discussions in the social media space. New technologies, from social media to iPads, are changing the way consumers interact with their brands. Dissatisfied customers are quick to express their frustrations on social media channels. Executives who don't know how these mediums operate can't respond to their clients' feedback because they can't see it in the first place. Nor could they implement guidelines for employee use of social media, which could result in employees misusing those media and causing marketing damage. And, if damage has already occurred, executives will need to understand how these tools work in order to respond quickly.

Without an understanding of the value of social media channels and new technology as marketing tools and revenue generators, executives are ill-prepared for the 21st century.

That's why I'm firmly convinced that business schools have a crucial role to play in familiarising the 50-plus age group to ensure that opportunities are fully exploited.

13

1	guidelines	reward	feedback
2	decide	manage	respond
3	answer	occur	reduce
4	digital	genuine	effective
5	customer	revenues	consumer
6	referrals	expenses	company

5 Employment trends

14

Now, in the next stage of my presentation, I'd like to focus on these two graphs. They both show the movements in employment levels in certain industries in a particular capital city and country in the period 1994–2010. The graph on the left shows the trends in the manufacturing industry, while the one on the right is about the service industry. As regards the manufacturing industry, the level of employment in the capital dropped significantly until 2007, even more so than in the country as a whole. There was a 30 per cent and a 15 per cent fall in the capital and in the country respectively. However, employment in the city rose dramatically by 15 per cent until mid 2010, then began falling again afterwards. By contrast, the national employment level rose steadily by 15 per cent from early 2008 till 2010.

As to the service industry, levels of employment fell by over 25 per cent in the capital and in the country as a whole. This increase happened very steadily at the national level but with several fluctuations in the capital city where, for example, a sharp increase from mid 2006 till the end of 2007 was followed by a rapid fall. From mid 2008, however, employment levels in the services have shown a clear upward trend in the capital.

15

Now, in the next stage of my presentation, I'd like to focus on these two graphs. They both show the movements in employment levels in certain industries in a particular capital city and country in the period 2004–2010. The graph on the left shows the trends in the manufacturing industry, while the one on the right is about the service industry. As regards the manufacturing industry, the level of employment in the capital dropped significantly until 2007, even more so than in the country as a whole. There was a 20 per cent and a 15 per cent fall in the capital and in the country respectively. However, employment in the city rose dramatically by 15 per cent until mid 2009, then began falling again afterwards. By contrast, the national employment level rose steadily by 15 per cent from early 2008 till 2010.

As to the service industry, levels of employment rose by over 25 per cent in the capital and in the country as a whole. This increase happened very steadily at the national level but with several fluctuations in the capital city where, for example, a sharp increase from mid 2006 till the end of 2007 was followed by a rapid fall. From mid 2009, however, employment levels in the services have shown a clear upward trend in the capital.

16

1	permanent	flexible	abusive
2	attrition	promotion	atmosphere
3	security	economy	motivation
4	location	company	loyalty

6 Ethics

17

Speaker 1: To recap on what we've decided, then. We will not take on any new admin staff on a permanent basis next year. Instead, we'll hire temps if and when the need arises.

Speaker 2: As I'm sure you're all aware, what we're here to talk about today is the stance of our new overseas supplier on environmental protection and work safety.

Speaker 3: Fine. Thank you all for your contributions. So to sum up it seems we're all agreed that the first step is to undertake a feasibility study.

Speaker 4: As you can see, the first item on the agenda today is our new corporate responsibility report. We'll have a look at what the competition has been doing in that area and see what we can learn from that.

Speaker 5: Now that we all have some background on the situation, perhaps Jimmy can tell us something about how they tackled a similar problem in Accounts last year.

Speaker 6: Right. It's gone 9.15 already so I suggest we make a start. Louise will kick off with some feedback on the conference she attended in Barcelona and then we'll see where we go from there.

Speaker 7: We've all heard the pros and cons of outsourcing all our computing work. Would anyone like to comment?

Speaker 8: We've called this meeting in order to reach a decision on whether any disciplinary measures need to be taken against our Deputy Sales Manager. You will remember that two complaints for harassment have already been lodged against him.

18

[**I** = Interviewer; **GT** = Goran Tielsen]

I With us in the studio this morning we have Goran Tielsen, author of *Markets, Money and Social Responsibility* and director of FSRI, the Forum for Socially Responsible Investment. Now Goran, allow me to go straight to the point: what *is* a socially responsible investor?

GT Well, a socially responsible investor is simply someone who cares about where their money goes. Like everyone else, socially responsible investors hope for a secure financial future but not at the expense of their moral, social or philosophical values. They expect the companies they invest in to reflect their values, to be socially, morally and environmentally responsible. They are investors and shareholders who expect more transparency and more accountability from companies and act to influence them towards social responsibility.

I So, to put it bluntly, they hope to make money, of course, but they also want to make a difference?

GT Yes, that's right. Although to be more precise the people we have in mind when we talk about socially responsible investors certainly do not only include shareholders. In fact, our forum brings together a majority of people whose money is invested by others.

I Such as?

GT Well, essentially high street banks, as well as pension funds. As regards the latter, for example, we encourage people to get as much information as possible on pension fund accounts. Anybody who contributes to a pension scheme is entitled to obtain details of the fund's shareholdings and the list of investments. Getting information is a necessary first step. It is only on the basis of accurate information that people can start campaigning for policy change.

I Could you say a few words about the social performance of pension funds?

GT Well, the picture is a rather complex one. We have found that a large number of funds, if not most funds, invest a certain percentage entirely ethically. However, it sometimes turns out that some of the very same funds have in their main portfolio a tobacco manufacturer or an arms-exporting company. What our forum can do in such cases is to organise our members into a group that will campaign for the exclusion of such companies from the portfolio.

I You also mentioned banks a few minutes ago.

GT Yes. It's not our forum that created the concept of ethical banking but we certainly pride ourselves on having made it gain such wide currency. We have done a great deal of research on the social and environmental behaviour of banks.

I And what does your research reveal?

GT We noted in particular that most leading banks needed to rethink their lending policies concerning environmentally sensitive projects. Our recommendations enabled some of the banks to take adequate measures and so preserve their reputation as ethical investors.

I Environmental issues obviously deserve a lot of our attention but what about issues such as Third World debt?

GT Mmm. The Third World debt crisis was at its height in the 1980s. Since then, however, most of the debt has been transferred to official creditors. All high street banks in this country have written off the bulk of their debts.

I So I suppose that's why Third World debt is no longer the focus of campaigns?

GT Exactly. Having said that, it is clear that a number of banks *do* still lend money to companies involved in controversial activities and also to countries with a poor human rights record. So current campaigns tend to focus more on those issues.

I How can a company's performance on human rights possibly be assessed?

GT That is extremely difficult indeed. In some cases it is practically impossible to make an adequate assessment. It seems reasonable to say that several countries would've improved their human rights record sooner if they had benefitted from investment instead of being boycotted. What matters is what the company *does* in such a country. One cannot assume that it automatically supports repression, it may well be a force for good, for development and change.

19

1 It could've been worse.
2 He must've been delayed.
3 She can't have lost it.
4 They wouldn't have done it.
5 I might've hit him!
6 You should've told me.

7 Finance

20

I am delighted to present my third report to shareholders as Chairman of Castel International following another year of strong performance.

Our company has consistently delivered superior total shareholder returns since its creation in 1989.

The results of the company were very strong and at the top end of the industry peer group. Net revenues rose by 9 per cent while net income rose by 22 per cent to €658m.

In May, the company announced its intention to return surplus cash to shareholders through a progressive dividend policy and a rolling share buyback programme. Both of these have been initiated. The interim dividend was increased by 8 per cent and the directors propose that the final dividend be increased by 7 per cent giving a total for the year of 40 cents a share, an overall increase of 12 per cent.

This dividend, if approved at the Annual General Meeting, will be paid on 30th March next year to shareholders on the register on 15th January.

At the same time, the company has begun its rolling share buyback programme and had already repurchased 2 million shares by the year end. It is the company's intention to proceed with this programme through next year.

21

[I = Interviewer; TA = Tricia Ashcroft]

I   Welcome to 'Business Today', our weekly programme in which we look at new business ideas and discuss the pains and joys associated with starting a new business. With us in the studio today is Tricia Ashcroft, president of the Yorkshire Association for Small Businesses. Hello Tricia.

TA Hi!

I   Tricia, in the latest edition of your Association's journal, you write that – allow me to quote you – 'Raising funds for a small business is close to impossible at the best of times, never mind in a recession.' Is that really so?

TA Absolutely. The crisis may have eased a little but the economy is still far from having picked up completely. Debt remains scarce and lenders are still reluctant to back new entrepreneurs, even those who seem to have a viable business idea.

I   What about banks?

TA Bob Hope, the great American comedian, once quipped 'A bank is a place that will lend you money if you can prove that you don't need it.' Now this may sound like a bit of an exaggeration – after all comedians are supposed to try and make us laugh – but I can assure you that I have met a lot of would-be entrepreneurs who confirm that all too often banks are reluctant to support innovative projects. Unless you already have capital to secure the loan, the banks generally aren't interested …

I   … which, of course, defeats the point.

TA Exactly.

I   When you say that banks 'generally' aren't interested, can we infer that there are exceptions?

TA Well, I'm glad you asked me that question. Yes, there are. The best example I can think of is Triodos, the ethical bank. They specialise specifically in supporting projects that have a positive impact socially or environmentally.

I   Mm. That sounds very interesting indeed. Erm … Right. So we've talked in general about the difficulties start-ups face. Let's consider now a specific example.

22

[I = Interviewer; TA = Tricia Ashcroft]

I   In your editorial, you describe in great detail the fascinating story of David and Vivien Bowen, the inventors of the 'green plug'. Could you give us the main points here?

TA Well, David and Vivien Bowen are in the clean technology sector, clean tech for short. Now, as I said earlier, access to capital is a problem for all industries but it is particularly affecting clean tech because this sector generally requires a huge amount of capital early on, erm, in the early stages, when money is needed for testing, experimenting, etc. In 2005, the Bowens came up with an idea for a 'green plug' that could turn off electrical appliances automatically, for example when you leave your iron accidentally switched on or when a machine is left on standby for long periods of time.

I   Mm. I could do with one of those. I think I'd save a lot of energy and money.

TA Yes. In fact, it's estimated that people would save over a pound a day on average! Well, despite all that, banks were not convinced and it took David and Vivien over a year to access venture capital. Besides, they were also turned down for government loans designed for green start-ups but …

I   Sorry to cut in on you, but how did they manage to raise the capital they needed, then?

TA Well, eventually, in late 2006, they found a business angel willing to invest £10,000 and that's how Logicor was born. Since then, the firm has raised over £3m, mainly through family, friends and angels.

I   And, of course, Logicor today is a successful company …

TA Yes and a very innovative one as well. Saving energy and resources is really what's at the core of their thinking.

I   Thank you, Tricia. Our listeners often turn to us for help and advice on how to deal with climate change by reducing energy consumption. For more information on Logicor's amazing energy-saving products, go to www.logicoruk.com, that's www.logicoruk.com.

8 Consultants

23

Speaker 1: Of course there are occasions when you want advice from someone who can take a detached view but that's certainly not always necessary. Halfway through the training one of our junior managers came up to me and told me how he would've loved to run such a workshop and why had I not asked him. So I looked at his resumé again, just to find out that yes, indeed, he seemed equally qualified and at least as experienced as the expert we'd brought in. But it was too late. What happened was, he handed in his notice shortly afterwards. Demotivation, I suppose.

Speaker 2: I still don't understand how it could have happened. I was certain absolutely everything had been discussed in great detail. It was only when I received the invoice that I realised the problem. You see, this particular consultant had worked for a couple of large corporations before and it seems there are so many things she just took for granted. She was used to having almost everything covered, business class travel, deluxe hotels and what have you. So that year my department overspent by over £1,000!

Speaker 3: I agree it would be unreasonable to expect consultants to work for you exclusively. Sooner or later they are bound to be hired by one of your competitors and, I hasten to say, that's not unprofessional. What we failed to do – and we've only got ourselves to blame for that – is spell out in writing that any information about the company gained during the consultancy mustn't be divulged under any circumstances. It turned out that at the time another person from the same consultancy firm was working for our main competitor so they repositioned their main brand in very much the same way as we did ours but two months before we did.

Speaker 4: Our employees are usually very cooperative, excellent team players all of them. Unfortunately things were quite hectic here at the time these two consultants started working for us. So most of our staff didn't have the faintest idea of who these two newcomers were or why they wanted to have a private discussion with everyone or why they requested access to certain files, etc, etc. Within less than a week, the tension was evident everywhere. Our employees felt threatened just because they didn't know what to expect.

Speaker 5: Sustainability is not just an empty buzzword. Most businesses want to function effectively without outside experts. We had to bring in one consultant after another. Things were always fine during the projects but, once they were over, it was back to square one. We weren't any better off as we still couldn't do the work for ourselves. It was all terribly frustrating and demoralising. It may have been good business for the consultants but for us it was unbearable. We felt as if we no longer had the power to run our business on our own.

24
1 I'll see what I can do.
2 I suppose I could look into it.
3 I think that should be doable.
4 I'll wait to hear from you then.
5 I'd have to check with my supervisor first.
6 She'd have to confirm the payment terms, you see.
7 I was wondering if you could deliver a bit sooner.
8 Maybe we could talk a little about payment terms at this point?

25
1 I'd agree to their terms if I were you.
2 If I'd been better prepared, I'd have felt more confident.
3 The project might've been successful if we'd set a more realistic timescale.
4 I don't think we'll be able to solve our problems unless we hire an independent consultant.
5 If he'd been a better communicator, I'm sure he'd have been asked to conduct the negotiation.
6 If they're genuinely concerned about those difficulties, they'll bring in a consultant.

9 Strategy

26
1 my office
2 try again
3 they arrived
4 we agreed
5 pay off
6 free enterprise

27
1 They agreed to come to my office.
2 Would May or June be all right?
3 Let's try again in a day or two.

28
1 A: The team members aren't particularly cooperative.
  B: But they are <u>creative</u>.
2 A: The team members aren't particularly creative.
  B: But they <u>are</u> creative.

29
1 A: Thanks for that book on strategic planning. Great stuff!
  B: I <u>thought</u> you'd like it.
2 A: That book isn't worth the paper it's printed on.
  B: I thought you'd <u>like</u> it.
3 A: The management can't be held responsible for this failure.
  B: Well, I believe the management <u>is</u> responsible.
4 A: Who would you say is to blame for this failure?
  B: Well, I believe the <u>management</u> is responsible.
5 A: Do they show any cynicism about the idea?
  B: Yeah. I find them <u>very</u> cynical.
6 A: So you're disappointed with our new team members?
  B: Yeah. I find them very <u>cynical</u>.
7 A: Does the new product appeal to teenagers?
  B: I'm afraid it has <u>no</u> appeal to teenagers.
8 A: Which segment doesn't find our new product appealing, then?
  B: I'm afraid it has no appeal to <u>teenagers</u>.

10 Online business

30
Bar chart 1
a) As we can see from this chart, the number of access points in 2009 wasn't as high in France as it was in Sweden or in the UK.
b) In 2009, there were about three times as many public access points in France as in the UK.
c) There were over twice as many public access points in Sweden as in France.

Bar chart 2
a) Of the three groups under consideration, French users are least affected by credit card abuse, spamming and viruses.
b) As we can see from this graph, the percentage of users experiencing security problems is considerably higher in the UK than in Sweden or France.
c) The percentage of users experiencing security problems in Sweden is significantly lower than in the UK or in France.

Bar chart 3

a) In 2008, approximately the same percentage of businesses offered formal IT training to their staff in France and Sweden.

b) The percentage of the workforce with IT training in France is only slightly lower than in Sweden or the UK.

c) By the end of 2008, a higher proportion of people in employment in the UK had benefited from IT training than anywhere else in Europe.

Bar chart 4

a) In 2010, broadband access for small businesses was almost three times as expensive in Italy as it was in Canada.

b) Although much cheaper than in Italy, broadband access for small businesses in Canada is still more expensive than in Germany.

c) In all European countries except Italy, broadband access is cheaper than in Canada.

Bar chart 5

a) As this bar chart shows, the connection speed in Italy is extremely slow and even more so in Germany.

b) You can connect twice as quickly in Canada as in Germany and 25 times as quickly as in Italy.

c) Although the connection speed in Germany is slow compared to Canada and Italy, it reaches 2.5 gigabytes per second.

Bar chart 6

a) Mobile phone use is more or less equally expensive in the three countries under scrutiny.

b) As you can see from this bar chart, although the cost of mobile phone use is much higher in Canada than in Italy, it is still lower than in Germany.

c) The cost of mobile phone use is considerably lower in Italy than in Canada.

11 New business

31

1 A: ... So the reference number of the invoice is 47/AP.
   B: Sorry, no. 47/<u>I</u>P.

2 A: ... and you are saying your original order was for forty units.
   B: No, no. It was four<u>teen</u> units. One four.

32

1 A: Let me just go over that. The supplier's name was Rod Jowett. J-O-W-E-double T.
   B: No. The surname's spelt J-O-W-<u>I</u>-double T.

2 A: ... and you said you expected delivery by June the third, is that right?
   B: No. In fact, delivery was due on June the <u>first</u>. So it's already three days late.

3 A: I just need to enter your details on my computer. So, Edmond Keeler, E-D-M-O-N-D ...
   B: Sorry. My first name is spelt E-D-M-<u>U</u>-N-D.

4 A: So you are saying that the invoice is three weeks overdue for payment.
   B: Well, no. I'm afraid it's already <u>five</u> weeks overdue.

5 A: The documents will be ready by Thursday as you requested.
   B: Sorry. It's on <u>Tuesday</u> that I need them.

6 A: So your office number is 064 735 458.
   B: No, 735 4<u>9</u>8.

12 Project management

33

[I = Interviewer]

I If I remember correctly, you issued your invitation to tender last December. What's been going on since?

CEO Well, the closing date for replies was exactly a week ago, March 31st that is. In those three months, 24 companies sent us their technical and cost proposals in the areas of computer reservation system services and Internet applications.

I Twenty-four! Did you expect that many?

CEO In fact, it's a lot more than we expected ...

I Can you comment on the proposals at this stage?

CEO All we can say at this point is that we are extremely pleased with the content and quality of all the proposals which we received. I repeat: all of them.

I So I assume you now have a tough task ahead?

CEO A tough one indeed! We've now got to start the evaluation stage, as you might expect. We've already formed an Evaluation Committee, whose task will be to review all 24 proposals so they can analyse costs, seek functional demonstrations and meet key management staff of the companies that bid.

I How long will that take?

CEO We expect the whole process to take about two months.

I And then?

CEO If all goes well, we should be able to award contracts in the first half of June.

I Thank you very much for these details. We're all looking forward to the decisions of the Evaluation Committee.

34

1 I need to make␣a list␣of␣all␣attendees.
2 Let's decide␣on what␣options we'll use for␣our call.

35

1 I'm␣afraid␣I haven't been␣able to create␣an␣agenda for the conference.
2 I don't like␣it when people bring␣up␣an␣issue which␣isn't␣on the agenda.
3 I contacted␣everyone␣and gave them the date␣and time␣of the teleconference.
4 I'd␣provided␣everyone with␣a lot␣of supplementary material well␣in␣advance.
5 It's␣always␣a nice␣addition to have some biographical␣information␣about the participants.

36

1	suc<u>cess</u>ful	im<u>por</u>tant	<u>sen</u>sible
2	<u>diff</u>icult	ef<u>fec</u>tive	ex<u>ter</u>nal
3	re<u>sour</u>ces	ob<u>jec</u>tive	<u>con</u>sequence
4	<u>o</u>verview	<u>qua</u>lity	de<u>ci</u>sion
5	<u>mo</u>tivate	de<u>li</u>ver	<u>or</u>ganise

Appendix

37

The sounds of English

See page 95.

Appendix

Shadowing is a very effective way to make the most of the recorded material.
1 Play a short section, i.e., a few words or one line of a dialogue, then pause.
2 Without speaking, repeat internally what you heard.
3 Play the same section again. Pause and speak the words in exactly the same way and at the same speed. Repeat this step until you are satisfied with your performance.
4 Play the same section again and speak along with the voice on the recording. This is shadowing.
5 Move on to the next short section of the recording and repeat the above procedure.

THE SOUNDS OF ENGLISH

◀))) **37 Look, listen and repeat.**

Vowel sounds

/ɪ/	quick fix
/iː/	clean sheet
/e/	sell well
/æ/	bad bank
/ɑː/	smart card
/ɒ/	top job
/ɔː/	short course
/ʊ/	good books
/uː/	school rules
/ʌ/	much luck
/ɜː/	first term
/ə/	aˈbout ˈCanada

Diphthongs

/eɪ/	play safe
/aɪ/	my price
/ɔɪ/	choice oil
/aʊ/	downtown
/əʊ/	go slow
/ɪə/	near here
/eə/	fair share

Consonants

1 Contrasting voiceless and voiced consonants

Voiceless		Voiced	
/p/	pay	/b/	buy
/f/	file	/v/	value
/t/	tax	/d/	deal
/θ/	think	/ð/	this
/tʃ/	cheap	/dʒ/	job
/s/	sell	/z/	zero
/k/	card	/g/	gain
/ʃ/	option	/ʒ/	decision

2 Other consonants

/m/	mine	/n/	net	/ŋ/	branding	/h/	high
/l/	loss	/r/	rise	/w/	win	/j/	year

Tips
- Identify the sounds that you have difficulty recognising or producing and focus mainly on these.
- Add your own key words in the tables above for the sounds you wish to focus on.
- Using the pause button on your CD player will give you time to speak or write when you do the exercises.

Pearson Education Limited

Edinburgh Gate, Harlow
Essex, CM20 2JE, England
and Associated Companies throughout the world

www.pearsonelt.com

First published 2006
Third edition 2011
ISBN: 978 1 4082 3704 5
Second impression 2013

Set in: MetaPlus 9.5/13.5
Printed in Malaysia (CTP-PPSB)
Project Managed by Chris Hartley

Acknowledgements
*We are grateful to the following for permission to reproduce
copyright material:*

Figures
Figure on page 63 adapted from International e-Commerce
Benchmarking Experimental Statistics Database, http://
www.statistics.gov.uk, Crown Copyright material is
reproduced with permission under the terms of the
Click-Use License.

Text
Extract on page 7 adapted from The careerist: First
impressions by Rhymer Rigby, published 12 March
2010 www.ft.com/cms/s/0/0A3f019c-2e19-11df-b85c-
00144feabdco.html#axzz19t1FjyWs, with permission from
the author; Extract on page 12 adapted from Miles away
from home but much closer to my goals by Laura Huang
published 17 January 2005, http://www.ft.com, with
permission from the author; Extract on page 13 adapted
from Our view of mentoring, http://www.astrazeneca.co.uk,
with permission from AstraZeneca; Extract on page 31
adapted from Why competent management means happy
workers, *Financial Times*, 07/04/2005 (Donkin, R.), with
permission from Richard Donkin, author of The Future of
Work, RichardDonkin.com; Extract on page 56 after Mission
Statement, http://www.adidas-group.com/en/ourgroup/
values/default.aspx, with permission from adidas AG;
Extract on page 56 after Mission Statement, www.vodafone.
com, © Vodafone Group; Extract on page 66 adapted from
It helps to look for a way out from the start, *Financial Times*,
29/06/2005 (Richard, D.), with permission from Douglas
Richard; Extract on page 67 adapted from Advice straight
from the dragon's mouth, *Financial Times*, 25/05/2005
(Richard, D.), with permission from Douglas Richard; Extract
on page 90 adapted from Older executives must master new
technology by Bettina Buchel published 20 August 2010,
Financial Times http://www.ft.com/cms/s/0/dc46029e-
ac6d-11df-8582-00144feabdco.html, with permission from
the author.

The Financial Times
Extract on page 17 adapted from Why the oil price rise
does not yet threaten crisis, *Financial Times*, 16/03/2005
(Andrew Balls, Ralph Atkins and David Pilling); Extract
on page 18 adapted from Nuclear energy: Come-back
kid or ugly duckling? by Fiona Harvey, 14 October 2004,
http://news.ft.com/cms/s/d2035268-1c28-11d9-bb5b-
00000e2511c8,dwp_uuid=c2f5b89c-184a-11d9-8963-
00000e2511c8.html; Extract on page 19 adapted from
Companies bow to pressure on emissions, *Financial Times*,
15/09/2005 (Harvey, F.); Extract on page 30 adapted from
The puzzle of the lost women, *Financial Times*, 01/03/2005
(Maitland, A.); Extract on page 35 adapted from Ethics: this
time it's personal, *Financial Times*, 24/03/2005 (Maitland,
A.); Extract on page 41 adapted from A third of Britons using
savings to supplement income by Jun Merrett, published 23
August 2010, http://www.ft.com/cms/s/2/ebfc844c-aeac-
11df-9f31-00144feabdco.html; Extract on page 47 adapted
from Boards are doing it for themselves, *Financial Times*,
18/05/2005 (Waldmeir, P.); Extract on page 55 adapted from
Marketing and business books: The targeting of Japan's
young tribes, *Financial Times*, 14/10/2004 (Sanchanta, M.);
Extracts on page 60, page 61 after Management metaphors
are truly out for the count by Lucy Kellaway published 2
March 2009 http://www.ft.com/cms/s/0/da3278d2-06cb-
11de-abof-000077b07658.html#axzz19ycQ6owF; Extract on
page 72 adapted from Why heroic feats are so rare, *Financial
Times*, 11/07/2005 (Stern, S.).

In some instances we have been unable to trace the
owners of copyright material, and we would appreciate any
information that would enable us to do so.